FRANCE

FRANCE

By
PIERRE MAILLAUD

Foreword by
D. W. BROGAN

Second edition

GEOFFREY CUMBERLEGE
OXFORD UNIVERSITY PRESS
LONDON   NEW YORK   TORONTO

Oxford University Press, Amen House, London, E.C.4

GLASGOW NEW YORK TORONTO MELBOURNE WELLINGTON
BOMBAY CALCUTTA MADRAS CAPE TOWN

Geoffrey Cumberlege, Publisher to the University

First Edition	1942
Second Impression	1943
Second Edition	1945
Second Impression	1947
Third Impression	1948
Fourth Impression	1950
Fifth Impression	1951

PRINTED IN GREAT BRITAIN

CONTENTS

CHAP.   PAGE

FOREWORD BY D. W. BROGAN 5

INTRODUCTION 7

I

THE MAKING OF FRANCE AND THE FRENCH PEOPLE

I. FRANCE AND HER EMPIRE IN 1939 . . . 11

II. THE FORTUNES OF FRANCE 20

III. THE FRENCH PEOPLE 38

IV. THE FRENCH MIND AND FRENCH CULTURE . . 48

II

THE FRENCH CRISIS IN THE TWENTIETH CENTURY

V. DEMOGRAPHIC POWER AND INTERNATIONAL POLICY 66

VI. TRADITIONAL ASSETS TURNED INTO LIABILITIES . 75

VII. AN ENDEMIC REVOLUTION 83

VIII. INTELLECTUAL AND MORAL HAMLETISM . . 93

IX. THE FRENCH DEFEAT 103

X. UNDER THE GERMAN HEEL 111

XI. ENGLAND AND FRANCE 127

INDEX 135

ILLUSTRATIONS

                                             PAGE

I. WOMEN WORKERS 19

II. TYPES OF FRENCHMEN 37

III. AMIENS CATHEDRAL 49

IV. IN THE FIELDS 73

V. CONSTRUCTION 79

VI. PEACEFUL FRANCE 95

VII. IN PARIS 125

VIII. FRANCE WILL RISE AGAIN 129

MAPS

                                             PAGE

FRANCE AND THE FRENCH COLONIAL EMPIRE, 1939 10

PARTITION OF CHARLEMAGNE'S EMPIRE, A.D. 843 . 12

OCCUPIED AND UNOCCUPIED FRANCE, 1940 . . 64

A la mémoire de mon frère Robert
tombé le 10 juin 1940
devant l'ennemi

FOREWORD

IN the picture of the world of to-day that this series attempts to give, failure to give a picture of France would be a great mistake, but not an unpardonable error. For France, in 1942, is largely *terra incognita*. For the first time since the Europe of the twelfth century went to school in Paris, the voice of France, in France, is mute. Real France is gagged and the official spokesmen of Paris and Vichy are ventriloquist's dummies. It is one of the most odious of Nazi triumphs. All the more necessary is it that Frenchmen outside France, Frenchmen to whom free speech is possible, should try to give the world an account of the causes of the present obscene spectacle of France in chains. And at the beginning of the third year of captivity, it is fitting that Oxford, the oldest child of the University of Paris, should enable a Frenchman to speak.

M. Maillaud, in his close-packed pages, has said a great many things that recall old truths and give a new form to them. The fact that all through her history France has had to 'live dangerously' is a truth that we are less likely to ignore after this war than after the last. That France, in 1939, was at her lowest point of energy was a fact known to the conspirators against civilization in Berlin; it was also known to the French people. Some of the causes of that weakness were transitory; some were comparatively old. M. Maillaud has, with great skill, distinguished between the two types of weakness. He has not only made plain the political and psychological consequences of the dreadful blood-letting of 1914–18, but the consequences, in modern war, of the cherishing of the peasant that has been the policy of the rulers of France for generations past. To her balance of industry and agriculture, France largely owed the variety of her civilization, the stability of her social order, the manifold attractions that made her the second country of all civilized men. But she owed her military weakness, too, in great part to that careful fostering of a peasant economy. For this is a true iron age and to ignore the fact that a predominantly agricultural economy cannot wage war, even defensive war, is to live in a world of pastoral poetry, not in the world in which our lot has been cast.

'Felix qui potuit rerum cognoscere causas'

wrote the greatest of pastoral poets, and the causes of the great disaster of the enslavement of France are made intelligible here. The grim story that is told is not one that makes for irremediable despair. 'France, mère des arts, des armes, et des loix', is not dead although captive. The causes of her captivity are set out here with the clarity and elegance that befits the subject. The causes of French captivity are not permanently effective and the liberation that we all await will be more than a deliverance of France, it will be a deliverance of Europe and of the world, unaccustomed to the unnatural silence that the barbarian has managed, for a brief space, to impose.

D. W. BROGAN

July 1942

INTRODUCTION TO THE FIRST EDITION

MANY short-term explanations have been given of what is often called 'the French collapse'. Perhaps it is still too early to expect any effort to place these events in their historical context. Considered judgement depends upon perspective, while passion and expediency jump to hasty comment. This is the age of the eye-witness, the monster of the twentieth century. Scores of scholars are still sorting out dusty evidence to find the true interpretation of Hannibal's failure before Rome or of the fall of Byzantium. But, thanks to the eye-witness and his miraculous gift of drawing positive conclusions from a week spent in the best hotel between the bar and the telephone-box, we may secure at the cost of a few shillings a complete analysis of every European crisis coupled with a recipe for a lasting cure. Thus the causes of the French 'collapse' were pointed out with an unerring finger by dozens of amateurs in diagnosis.

Against some of these versions, which smack of scandal-mongering rather than of serious study, I have tried to set up an image of France, not in 1939 or 1940 only, but of France as a national body which has weathered many crises, which has alternately known high achievement and deep depression.

More than any other country France blends with her own characteristics the reflections of a changing world. Less than any other can she remain impervious to external influences. More than any other she has given and received. As a consequence of her geographical situation, she is the most exposed country in the world. D'Annunzio's famous motto: 'Live dangerously' best defines her physical and moral destiny.

Of that destiny the tragedy of 1940 is but an episode. This military catastrophe will so prove when set against its historical background, however much many Englishmen may be tempted to speak of finality, in the face of a French defeat which left them almost alone in the midst of a desperate struggle.

I have tried to record in the present book some of the antecedents (I dare not say causes) of the defeat and of the French reaction to it, and to show that it was related to a process of development in France and in Europe, the effect of which counted for more than the mistakes or shortcomings of a few men.

I have no other qualification for this task than my faith in my own country's mission and my profound belief in its power to resume it. Both have at least encouraged me to consider the French problem with more care and attention than a casual

traveller could bring to bear on it. They have also safeguarded
me against versions of the events of 1940 which belong to the
realm of fiction or of spicy gossip. The *Chronique de l'Œil de
Bœuf* may be an interesting sidelight on the reign of Louis XIV,
but only in so far as it remains a sidelight and is not presented
as a basis for historical study, for it can explain neither its
greatness nor even some of its failures. I cannot, for instance,
accept the relationship between a French Prime Minister and
a woman in French society as even a partial explanation of a
national crisis, nor can I ascribe to the influence of a few paltry
journalists the temporary eclipse of a mighty civilization.
Many aspects of French public life may have been symptoms
of some disease. But in themselves they supply no explanation.
Worse symptoms have been evident at other times and produced no such effect. Louis XIV once deserted his post at the
head of the French army in the Low Countries to spend a few
days with Madame de Montespan, an act of desertion of which
M. Paul Reynaud would have been utterly incapable. But the
social, economic, and military strength of France at that time
remained completely unaffected by such individual lapses.
Talleyrand, who rescued France from the pit into which
Napoleon had hurled the nation, was the same unscrupulous
cynic who, on his first appointment as Foreign Minister, had
stepped into his state coach with the words: 'At last, here's
a good chance to make money.' The presence in public life
of excessive elements of weakness or even corruption is not a
cause but an effect. Moreover, it depends on context and
background whether or not bad symptoms in the life of a country
disturb its national development. A cold harmless enough
to a sound constitution will aggravate the condition of a man
in advanced consumption.

  The factors which determined the defeat of France are
broader and deeper than those suggested by writers whose
knowledge of her was based on a brief and probably unpleasant
acquaintance, or by political partisans, or even by men whose
lifelong purpose was fulfilled when they found an international
atmosphere particularly receptive to a condemnation of France
in the eyes of friendly nations.

  At the same time there is nothing final in the eclipse of
France. The very process of evolution and transformation
which she was undergoing when she was struck down and which
made her defeat the more complete, is in itself an assertion of
national vitality. Because the traditional capacity of France to
show her resilience in emergency was not apparent in 1940,
many of her friends were led to believe that it was extinguished.
And they were all the more inclined to accept the facile thesis

of her decadence because she had disappointed the hopes of England and left her in deadly peril. But the surge of national energy cannot always coincide with the time of the greatest need nor does it inevitably correspond to the demands of a great human cause. Yet the revival will come, and its fore-shadowing signs are already clear even under the German yoke.

Against the notion of finality and the thesis of French decadence I shall invoke arguments which can best be indi-cated in this introduction by a comparison. The fate of France, as I see it, may be likened to a Shakespearean drama, whereas the prophets of French decadence would regard it as a Greek tragedy. Greek tragedy is an assertion of finality. It has a beginning and an end. When the cycle is completed, there is nothing more to expect, nothing more to hope. When Oedipus dies, everything dies with Oedipus. In Shakespeare there is no finality. Beyond individual destiny he suggests develop-ment and yet continuity. Hamlet's death does not close the book, nor does it interrupt the process of thought. Even as darkness descends upon the stage, the light surges from the background with the appearance of Fortinbras, who is not so much a conqueror as a challenge to finality.

On the French stage, where darkness had descended in June 1940, the first lights soon arose after a tragic episode, lifted above a trampled earth by the humblest men, as beacons of hope, as tokens of faith, as heralds of the dawn which could not fail to come. It has come now. A day of toiling, of supreme exertion, has begun. But life has resumed its course.

P.M.

April 1942

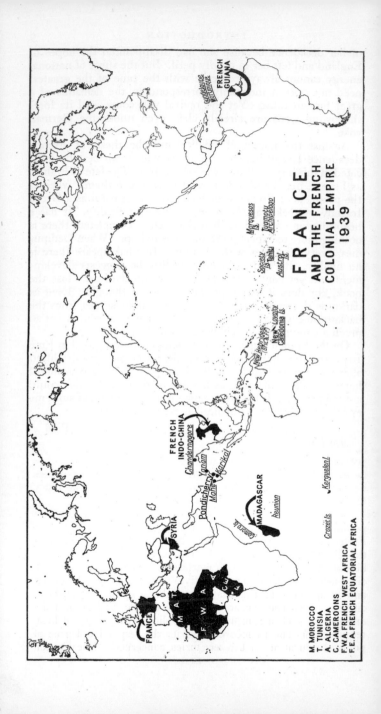

FRANCE
AND THE FRENCH
COLONIAL EMPIRE
1939

FRENCH GUIANA

Guadeloupe Martinique

Marquesas Is.
Tuamotu Archipelago
Society Is.
Tahiti Austral

New Hebrides
New Loyalty
Caledonia Is.

Kerguelen I.

FRENCH
INDO-CHINA
Chandernagore
Yanáon
Pondicherry
Mahe Karikal

MADAGASCAR
Comoro Is.
Reunion

Crozet Is.

FRANCE
SYRIA

F.W.A.
F.E.A.

M. MOROCCO
T. TUNISIA
A. ALGERIA
C. CAMEROONS
F.W.A. FRENCH WEST AFRICA
F.E.A. FRENCH EQUATORIAL AFRICA

I. THE MAKING OF FRANCE AND THE FRENCH PEOPLE

CHAPTER I

FRANCE AND HER EMPIRE IN 1939

THE French Republic in 1939 was a state of some forty-two million inhabitants, including three million foreigners. The French-born population did not exceed the figure of 1913, despite the recovery of Alsace-Lorraine, with its 1,900,000 inhabitants, and some slight immigration from over-seas territories. Both went to make up for the enormous drain of blood in the years 1914–18. On the whole, between 1919 and 1939, the number of births barely offset the number of deaths.

Metropolitan France covers an area of 212,660 square miles. The density of the population is two and a half times lower than that of Great Britain, whose forty-five million inhabitants live on an area of 90,000 square miles. France, which was the second state in Europe in area, was only the fifth in population. In agricultural production she came second after the U.S.S.R.; in industrial power she was behind Germany, Great Britain, and the U.S.S.R.

Being an imperial power, her resources could not, however, be exactly assessed on the mere basis of a comparison with those of a few continental nations. The French colonial Empire, which spreads over four continents, is the second largest in the world in area (5,150,000 square miles), the third in population (about sixty-three millions). Its widest stretches lie in the most desert regions of Africa. The richest colonies border the sea: Algeria, Morocco, Tunis, Dahomey, the Ivory Coast, Senegal, the West Indies, Indo-China.

The situation of France in Europe and her relatively low population, together with the principles inherited from the French Revolution, were responsible for the colonial policy of the French Republic, which was unquestionably the most liberal in the world in all matters of assimilation. French citizenship was granted to all natives who discharged the duties and obligations to the State incumbent upon French-born citizens. It is true that administrative caution had to limit the excesses of such a comprehensive policy, in the light of local requirements and in accordance with the respective degree of political education in the territories concerned. The French

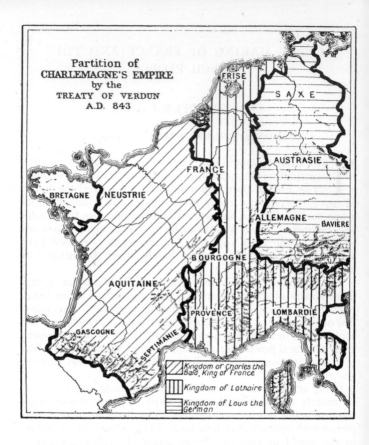

Partition of
CHARLEMAGNE'S EMPIRE
by the
TREATY OF VERDUN
A.D. 843

FRISE

SAXE

AUSTRASIE

FRANCE

BRETAGNE   NEUSTRIE

ALLEMAGNE   BAVIERE

BOURGOGNE

AQUITAINE

PROVENCE   LOMBARDIE

GASCOGNE

SEPTIMANIE

Kingdom of Charles the Bald, King of France
Kingdom of Lothaire
Kingdom of Louis the German

administration succeeded on the whole in maintaining the validity of its liberal principles, and in encouraging legitimate aspirations while preserving the white population against an overdose of coloured blood.

The result was a very high standard of allegiance to France throughout her colonial Empire. The loyalty of the native populations has survived the European defeat so completely and so strikingly that neither the weakening of the central authority nor the ceaseless efforts made by Germany and Italy to provoke disaffection have been able to impair their allegiance to France. Whether under Vichy or under Free French rule, the effects of the Republic's colonial policy have endured. The importance of this phenomenon cannot be over-emphasized in a world where every factor of stability must be preserved and strengthened.

Lyautey, the greatest of all French colonial administrators, has left to the French nation a short sentence which defines a vast policy: 'France is a nation of a hundred million inhabitants.'

These words were not only a reminder of the resources of the Empire. They were a warning to France that, henceforth, her position in Europe would depend to a large extent upon the exploitation of her Empire; that France, as a continental power only, had ceased to enjoy the privileged position which she had held for many centuries, thanks to her relatively large population. And they were a challenge to French insularism: an insularism of a peculiar type, for the French had always been conscious of Europe. But the majority of the people were less acutely aware of their Empire. Yet it was a signal defeat in Europe, in 1871, which developed in the French *élite* a sense of imperial power. Indeed, this sense, which had grown as a result of a continental threat, created a form of Empire-mindedness very different from that of other countries. For the French, the human contribution made by the Empire had as much value as its economic resources. Even in the Empire, France was still thinking of the Rhine frontier. So was Lyautey when he reminded his fellow countrymen that France was a nation of a hundred million inhabitants. The latest chapters of French colonial conquest are still comparatively recent. At the beginning of the present century, to the vast majority of Frenchmen, the conquest remained an epic, a page of glory and adventure rather than a practical enterprise. It opened a new field to military initiative and a good training school for energy and character. The exploitation of the Empire did not appear to the average man as a vital necessity, because his essential requirements could be otherwise satisfied. Until 1914, the majority of the French nation remained an essentially continental people thinking in terms of its metropolis, thriving on the most favoured land in Europe, well content with it, and periodically compelled to pay a tribute of blood to protect its land, its harvests, and its national way of life.

Just as the Franco-Prussian War had stimulated imperial conquest, the first World War brought home to a large number of Frenchmen the importance of their Empire in a tangible form, the appearance on various fronts of troops drawn from this vast reservoir of man-power. Since then the realization of the Empire's strategic value and potentialities has grown. Several campaigns in Syria and Morocco against rebellious tribes, the large number of conscripts who spent their time of military service overseas and the success of many business concerns in North and West Africa, increased the contacts

B

of every class of the population with the colonies and the
general knowledge of colonial matters. The imperial tradition was upheld by a strong body of civil servants and even
more by a powerful colonial army.

In 1939, France was therefore on her way to becoming a
very closely knit Empire. The very fact that the Reynaud
government had decided to remove to Algeria (although this
decision was annulled by its successor) is very significant. For
such a decision bears no relation to that of any British government in similar circumstances. The French Empire is a
colonial Empire and not a Commonwealth of nations of French
blood. Entrusting the fate of French institutions to territories
where the native populations overwhelmingly outnumber the
French, would have been a great departure from traditional
policy.

The division of opinion which this contemplated step provoked (apart from the dishonourable motives prompting a
number of politicians) is, however, an illustration of the conflict which persisted in French minds between two tendencies:
one natural, and the other acquired. The acquired one was
towards a more comprehensive conception of France. The
natural one was to consider that France remained on continental soil and that Antaeus-like, the French would lose their
strength and inspiration if their feet could not tread their
ancestral earth. The decisive part played by the French
Empire in the second World War between the Armistice and
the Allied landing in Normandy cannot fail decisively to influence the French imperial outlook in years to come and to
make every Frenchman Empire-conscious in a permanent and
active way.

But in the last twenty years, Empire-consciousness, although
it had very noticeably grown, had not done so to the extent of
making Lyautey's sentence an unqualified truth. Forty million
Frenchmen, before their country was struck down, were still
living at ease and with some elbow room in a wide and fertile
country. Such as it was, this land was still capable of development in every direction. Never had the French been compelled
to look with anxiety across the sea for their food supplies.
Never had they, like Antonio, waited till their ship came home
to fulfil their obligations. They could dig their good earth
and make it pay.

Geography has made France a natural economic unit, because of a diversity unparalleled in Europe. Indeed, the
combination of unity and diversity is perhaps the most distinctive feature of metropolitan France. The geographical
unity was somewhat naïvely acknowledged by a German pro-

fessor shortly after the last war when he remarked that 'any French child can draw from memory a fairly accurate map of his own country'. In fact, only the northern frontier (less than 400 miles out of nearly 3,500) might cause the child to hesitate over the drawing-paper: it is the only one not clearly defined by sea, mountain, or river. France's diversity is even more conspicuous. To this quality the Frenchman is very much alive, as well as to the singularity of this phenomenon in Europe, and the most uncouth French peasant will draw the foreigner's attention to its practical value.

This diversity expresses itself in every form: variety of produce, climate, scenery, people, habits, and traditions.

The temperature sometimes falls to 40 degrees of frost east of Besançon, in the most continental part of France, when it may well reach 58 degrees Fahrenheit in the most sheltered part of the Riviera, and the winter sports fans may open the skiing season in Mégève when the last bathers begin to shiver on the beach of St. Tropez.

The farmer of Flanders and Artois can grow sugar beetroot, whilst oranges are picked in Nice and tobacco leaves dried in Languedoc. Soon after millions of bushels of wheat have been harvested in the central plains of France, the orchards of Guyenne yield thousands of tons of peaches and plums. And when the last apples and pears of Normandy are gathered and crushed for cider, cartload after cartload of grapes redden or gild first the sunny roads of the Bordelais and then the lanes of Anjou and the hilly paths of Burgundy. Breton fishermen sail their frail fleets towards Newfoundland for cod-fishing while the richest cattle herds in Western Europe are being driven down from mountain to plain. Wood-cutters begin their hard tasks in the melancholy forests of Sologne when the shepherds of Savoy at the crack of dawn marshal their sheep away to some new pasture to graze 10,000 feet above sea-level.

Variety in habits, costume, and mood, is no less marked: as the first white-aproned waiter lifts the shutters of his small provincial café with his double-pronged pole, a peasant in a little church of Finistère, 300 miles away, is kneeling down to pray, his round black hat held against his stomach, an ivory cross dangling over his short velvet jacket, his baggy brown breeches spreading over the straw seat of his chair. At the same hour one of the belated revellers in Paris waves his top hat and white scarf to hail a racing taxi, whilst a cowboy of the Camargue carefully polishes his brand new maroquine riding-boots and star-shaped spurs to make his *début* on the Arles arena early in the afternoon.

These and other images of France are within the compass of

every schoolboy's memory or imagination. But this double notion of unity and diversity does not suffice to define the main characteristics of the French land. In order to complete the picture, another and very specifically French notion must be added: the notion of balance between these various elements. Two thousand years ago, Caesar compared France to a human body in which no organ is missing, of which no organ is superfluous. The balance between plain and mountain, between continental and maritime regions, between pastures and agricultural zones, between water and earth is so striking that it appears from a glance at a map. The accidents of terrain are nowhere so abrupt as to make any part of France uninhabitable. The system of waterways is one of the most complete and orderly in the world. It never falls short of the need nor does it anywhere exceed it.

Rivers have played a great part in the life and development of France. Within her frontiers, they serve as a guide to the traveller. They show him where to look for mountains, where they widen and spread into the plains, inviting industry, luxury, and art, and where to find the main ports, like gates opening on the sea. Thanks to this unique system of waterways, nowhere turbulent and uncontrollable, and which has been improved by a number of canals, very few parts of France are deserted. It brings everywhere a sense of life active yet gentle, of strength within order and measure.

This is, no doubt, the reason why the most essentially French part of France's civilization was born on her rivers. Her most prosperous towns are built on them. Her finest cathedrals rise from their banks. The turrets of her most graceful castles are reflected in their waters. Her great economic regions are easily definable through them.

These great French waterways, from the Somme to the Garonne and the Rhone, had already sketched out the first map of France long before any policy of natural frontiers had been dreamt of. Perhaps it was no mere coincidence that the first French political thinker, Louis XI, in his castle of Plessis-Les-Tours, on the banks of the Loire, foresaw the French 'realm to be', one hundred years before Henri IV set out to achieve its unification. It was also from the banks of the Loire that a clearly marked French culture began to spread, as the heir and successor to the great Italian Age, less rich in art but greater in thought, since it broke away from the scholastic rule and ushered in modern ethics.

France has over two thousand miles of sea coast and approximately the same length of land frontiers. She lies between the Continent and the sea, firmly bound to the one and yet wide open to the other. Her unequalled network of rivers provides the links between land and sea. It is almost as though it symbolized the French compromise between the continental and the maritime extremes and perhaps the great dilemma in many French minds between a continental and an imperial policy.

The same quality of balance also appears in the distribution of the French population over the territory. Partly because of its harmonious geography and partly because of its system of waterways, the population of France is more evenly spread over the land than that of the other great European nations. Its density is naturally greater in the northern parts of the country, which contain most of the great industrial centres, with the exception of Le Creusot, Lyons, and St. Etienne. Besides, the expansion of trade during the nineteenth century increased the maritime population. But the process of concentration of population which has been a notable feature in world evolution during the last hundred years has been slower and more limited in France than elsewhere. In 1939, more than 55 per cent. of the population lived in hamlets or towns of less than 4,000 inhabitants. Problems of supply or accommodation which assail a country with a highly centralized and concentrated population, did not arise. Regional migration and especially national migration was never a necessity.

The French, therefore, in spite of their colonial conquests and of the progress of communications, were inclined to a sedentary life, not only nationally but also regionally. Travelling was a pleasure and a luxury rather than a need. Work, entertainment, or repose were never out of reach.

Paris had become an increasingly powerful magnet. But, although a hundred and fifty years of administrative and cultural centralization had reduced the political importance of provincial capitals, many towns in addition to Paris had remained, in various degrees, effective centres of gravitation. Either in seats of learning, or in monuments from the past, or in opportunity for work and enterprise, or in facilities for rest and entertainment, there was hardly a French province which was so deficient as to compel temporary or permanent exile.

Frenchmen did travel in recent years more than they had ever done in the past, and France's holiday rush was just as great and gregarious as any other: but the basic elements of contented life, material and spiritual, were still present in almost every part of France. Of this the French remained conscious, and sometimes even more so when they had travelled farther afield.

This capacity of the French land to gratify men's demands without imposing upon them the sacrifice of emigration or the hazards of a quest for new dwelling-places, is responsible for this strange saying which the Germans have coined in their language: *Glücklich wie Gott in Frankreich*—a saying which has had unfortunate effects.

It is true that in 1939, despite economic, social, and political crises, the country's great natural assets still made individual life in France happier than it had become in most parts of Europe. These assets, which were to prove heavy liabilities in terms of international power, still remained valuable in terms of 'life within the nation', even in the midst of profound and far-reaching changes.

But this 'French way of living', which the Germans envied as a boon undeserved by its possessors, was not merely the product of a fortunate land. It had been dearly bought. The riches and harmony of nature were a geographical fact; but its exploitation had been a human accomplishment repeatedly threatened from within and without. It was the work of human endeavour and suffering.

When the French defences broke down under the German onslaught and the German mechanized hordes were let loose over this fertile and flourishing land, it was not the first time that a civilization which has been and remains essential to the progress of Europe had been threatened with extinction.

Indeed this civilization had sprung from its physical and cultural struggle with Germany. Its birth, its crystallization, its radiation throughout Europe and the world, are inseparable from the national resistance of France to German nomadic instincts and tribal migrations. Its role as a guardian of Western culture has only been fulfilled through the centuries in so far as France was also able to perform the function of keeper of her own realm. In order to follow Candide's advice and to cultivate her garden, she had to use not only the spade but the sword on her frontiers and often within her frontiers.

In order to understand the real circumstances of the French defeat in 1940, to see it in its proper context, and to assess its implications, it is first necessary to recall some phases of France's long history, with its two thousand years of invasions, wars, dynastic and social changes, political and religious strife, bold enterprise and patient endeavour. Set against this historical background, the French crisis of the twentieth century can be judged in its true light and perspective.

I. WOMEN WORKERS

1. WASHING CLOTHES   2. LAND GIRLS
(*Paul Popper*)   (*Black Star*)

CHAPTER II

THE FORTUNES OF FRANCE

IN July 1941, at Mulhouse in Alsace, Dr. Summer, Administrative President for the Third Reich, made the following statement: 'Providence has placed the German people at the very heart of Europe and has entrusted us with the mission of establishing order in Europe. We shall wrest from those peoples who live on our *Lebensraum* such areas as we need to accommodate and feed not only ourselves but our posterity: namely 200 million [*sic*] Germans. And we shall drive out of these areas all the heterogeneous peoples.'

To many readers the purpose revealed in those words may seem like the fantasy of a dreamer. Yet it manifested itself in action sixteen hundred years before it was expressed in a verbal statement. Dr. Summer's speech is not a 'programme' in the accepted sense. It puts into words a basic German instinct which is described, in modern jargon, as *Expansionism*. His definition is in fact an understatement, for it sets a limit to the German migratory impulse, whereas that impulse is uncontrollable and therefore boundless. Any progress in German expansion can only stimulate it further.

Racialism supplied Hitler with a Map of German Expansion, namely, the chart of ancient migrations. The first step was to unite all Germans within and without the State, thus extending German control to those territories which did not lie within the State frontiers; the second, to find a *Lebensraum* for their needs according to historic or even prehistoric precedents; the third, to base further aggrandizement on ever-growing 'needs'. Such was the purpose of the pseudo-scientific racial theories which, like every conceivable form of research undertaken by the Germans, were designed merely as an offensive weapon.

Hitler is the true heir of the tribal migrators of the fifth century, the embodiment of 'centrifugal Germany'. Stripped of its perfervid vocabulary and soap-box philosophy, his policy is only a modern version of the German wandering instinct. If the initial process of German expansion and overflowing has ever been limited, checked, disciplined and even turned into an asset in the past, the world owes it to a number of counter-forces which prevented the blast of German centrifugal forces from wrecking a civilization born of the Greek, Roman, and Christian cultures. Of these forces the foremost has been France.

For many centuries past Frenchmen have seen, on the one hand, a country with laws, customs, and creeds, and, on the other, communities leading the nomadic and lawless existence of migrators, whose urge was to expand and to feed on the wealth accumulated by order and patience. It is true that the Germanic factor has played its part in the making of the French people, next after the Celtic and the Latin elements. Tamed and polished, it has proved a valuable addition. Yet Germany is like those chemicals of which a small dose is beneficial but a full dose fatal. For sixteen centuries France's history is identified with her struggle for self-preservation. For sixteen centuries French culture has developed and flourished in proportion to the degree of success attending that struggle. For sixteen centuries self-preservation has dictated to French statesmanship a policy which has endured and never changed even through dynastic and social upheavals, a policy with countless exponents: Philip Augustus, Saint Louis, Philippe le Bel, Louis XI, Henri IV, Richelieu, Louvois, Carnot, Guizot, the Cambons.

This policy has been alternately defensive and preventive. From the partition of Charlemagne's Empire in 843 to the time of Richelieu, its aim was to reclaim the lands lost by the dismemberment of that Empire. For eight hundred years France fought to protect against the foreign foe a realm patiently reconstructed, and she nearly collapsed for ever in the sixteenth century when Charles V of Habsburg gathered under his sceptre every one of the lands which surrounded her —an encirclement of which the twentieth century has provided a second example.

Richelieu's greatness lies in the fact that he evolved something more than a mere defensive policy: a preventive one. Its fundamental aim was to keep the peoples of Germany divided. This much-disputed principle is nothing more than a French version of the English system which is based on a 'balance of power'. It was as imperative for France to keep in a state of division the vast reservoir of men beyond the Rhine, whence so many invasions had started, as for England to prevent the establishment of a crushing combination of Powers on the Continent. If Richelieu's application of the principle of balance has often been condemned, it is because it was practised at the expense of what we now consider a single 'nation' and because it ran counter to the notion of nationalities as accepted in the nineteenth century. Yet this preventive method may have saved Europe two centuries ago from the effects of German unification, which the inevitable defeat of the Protestant princes by the Emperor made a certainty. As for the contention that German nationalism was born of the Thirty Years War, it is but one of the conflicting arguments by which

the Germans themselves justify an expansionism which existed
long before they had any national conceptions at all, for it is
basically a herd instinct. Germany's historical evolution bears
no resemblance to that of France or Britain. It proceeded
neither from a clear idea of 'the realm' (for the nomadic
wanderings of successive German tribes had blurred any such
concept), nor from a common religious and cultural patrimony
(for there was none between those German lands which had
been civilized by Rome and the tribal communities of barbarian Prussia), nor from an orderly notion of the State as a
way of life and a means of exchange between individuals (for
every progress in German unification has evinced a social
philosophy based on the *external* power of the State rather
than on its internal values). Unity in Germany has remained
gregarious rather than civic. It has always stimulated expansionism, because its real purpose was not the gathering in a
common realm of men ruled by peaceful and progressive laws,
but the rallying of warriors on a jumping-off ground for
migrations and external adventures. Complete German unity
in the racial sense, which is the sole conception of unity in the
German mind, was not achieved until 1938. Its consequences
certainly vindicate Richelieu's preventive policy.

By the Treaty of Westphalia in 1648, which was the posthumous outcome of Richelieu's diplomacy, German unity was
postponed for nearly three centuries. Although this diplomacy
has remained to this day a veritable charter for French statesmen, it was misunderstood during the eighteenth century,
when French policy for the first time lost sight of the true
German menace and was thus partly responsible for the
growth of the Prussian State as heir to the scheme of German
unification. This departure from tradition deserves special
attention, for it is an important chapter in French history.

All the aims of Richelieu's diplomacy, which comprised not
only the division of Germany but the weakening of Habsburg
power in Spain as well as in the East, were accomplished under
Louis XIV, whose reign probably marked the culmination of
French power in Europe. It was during that reign that the
realm was 'closed' by the acquisition of the Rhine and Vosges
frontier; yet, during its second part, the war against the coalition of England, Holland, the Emperor, Spain, and Savoy, and
especially the War of the Spanish Succession, had two effects,
the first being the rise of English power, the second the birth
of Prussia as a modern State, the child of the League of
Augsburg.

This double legacy from Louis XIV's reign had a serious
influence on French policy throughout the eighteenth century.

As a result of those wars, England stood as France's chief potential enemy. For the first time since the Treaty of Picquigny in 1477 France's attention turned towards the west and lost sight of continental evolution. This evolution was clear. The centre of gravity of Germany was drifting northwards from Austria to Prussia. Yet, in the War of the Austrian Succession, France strengthened Prussia by an alliance from which Frederick II withdrew as soon as he had reaped tangible profit in the annexation of Silesia. France 'had worked for the King of Prussia' and when, in the Seven Years War, French policy embarked upon the well-known 'reversal of alliances' and joined the Habsburgs against England and Prussia, she met an enemy whom she had strengthened with her own hands. The reversal of alliances, wise in itself, came too late. Not only was France outwitted and outfought overseas by England, but she had 'lost the scent' on the Continent. Austria, which had become a conservative force, remained unpopular in France despite the new alliance. The Prussian enemy remained almost popular by reason of the widespread myth of her 'cultural enlightenment'. Monarchist historians sometimes charge the French Revolution with having misjudged France's true foreign interests. Yet the confusion of issues came before the Revolution, which inherited heavy liabilities from a weakening régime lacking men of vision and purpose. As a maker of men, the monarchy was exhausted. Like Kipling's Akela, it lost its hold on its people when it missed its quarry.

Still, despite foreign misfortune and overseas losses, despite fiscal mismanagement and political caprice, it was in a powerful, rich, and resilient France that the great Revolution broke out in 1789. Administratively and politically, the French were less 'advanced' than the English. Intellectually, despite royal absolutism, the French community was already highly educated, and both Christian and liberal in outlook. France, as a civilization, was born in the Middle Ages, an era of far greater individual independence and initiative than is commonly believed. Her customs and traditions partook of the Roman Catholic habit of resignation to circumstances, as well as of a patriarchal conception of Society on the one hand, and of the liberal, individualistic, and critical tendencies of the French mind on the other. The belief that the Revolution turned an antiquated, obsolete, and retrograde people into a progressive and modern State is as naïve in its romantic interpretation of history as the idea, prevailing at the time, that the Revolution had turned France into a den of iniquity. When it broke out she had centuries of history behind her

She had already known many changes and adaptations. Her
foreign policy had had its greatest exponents. Her people had
accepted much, but questioned as much. France had had her
Renaissance, her Classical Age, her cultural reformers. She
had been Christian for nearly eighteen centuries, and had felt
the effects of two religious reformations, though she had, on
the whole, rejected both. Even under the reign of her most
absolute monarch, Louis XIV, she had known the rule of
commoners.

It was a full-grown people that took the Bastille.

Seen by its contemporaries, the great French Revolution
was like a hurricane uprooting the very foundations of French
political, social, and economic life. It substituted entirely new
values for all the old ones, threw traditions, habits, ideas into
the melting-pot out of which it produced a brand-new world.
Considered in its historical perspective, the main effect of the
Revolution on France from a social point of view was the
advance of a new class which had been striving to assert itself
for a century and a half and which was suddenly brought to the
forefront: the *bourgeoisie*. After the Revolution had been 'de-
canted', after it had withdrawn from its most extreme dogmatic positions, it was that class which eventually emerged
as the great victor. In the economic field, the tangible results
of the Revolution were a general redistribution of the land
and a consequent increase of the national income, thanks to a
more thorough exploitation of the soil and to the abolition of
inter-regional barriers to trade. Politically, it led to the direct
participation of the people in the management of public affairs.
For a long time this progress was beneficial only to the same
class, as the right to vote was granted only to property-owning
citizens. To that extent it may be said that the Revolution
strengthened among the French the instinct of property and
the belief in a close relationship between the notion of individual freedom and that of the right to possess. Administratively, the Revolution achieved a higher degree of centralization than had absolute monarchic power. Ideologically, the
consequences of the Revolution are more difficult to define.
It certainly developed national feeling and made patriotism a
permanent feature in the French individual character. More
generally, the 'Déclaration des Droits de l'Homme', and the
adoption of the famous trilogy: 'Liberté, Egalité, Fraternité',
left a legacy the importance of which it is far from easy to
assess. In 1789 one knew that it meant the abolition of privilege, equality of opportunity for all men, the right to participate in the administration of the country, freedom of speech,
the right of ownership, of public trial, and the like. Some

of the articles of this new code were innovations. Some had
been borrowed from the English Constitution and enlarged.
Some have not stood the test of time: thus the twentieth century has shown to what extent liberty and equality may be incompatible. The chief merit of the French Revolution lies
perhaps in the fact that it opened new channels of thought,
encouraged boldness in social and political conceptions, introduced a spirit of toleration, a disposition to consider without
prejudice all suggestions and possibilities, and, in a word, substituted political nonconformity for resignation in public life. The
effects of the revolution are far clearer in the mental and social
attitude which it engendered than in its ideological values.

Perhaps the active forces which, as a result of its fundamental dynamism, the revolutionary era unleashed within
France and throughout Europe, have had far greater historical
consequences than what are commonly termed 'the ideas of
1789'. It is certain for instance that the wars of Napoleon
influenced the destinies of Europe more than the 'Déclaration
des Droits de l'Homme'. Similarly, the catastrophic financial
inflation of the Revolution and Directory, to which a precedent
had been set by the bankruptcy of Law's system of credit
during the early years of the century, left a deeper mark on the
minds of the French peasants (although they benefited by it in
their purchases of land) than the principle of equality in taxation. From these crises originated the peasants' distrust of
any form or system of state and banking credit, which lasted
to the present day and restricted national exchanges.

The chief cause of confusion in most analyses of the French
Revolution is this: whereas the most spectacular antecedents
of the social changes were the writings of philosophers and
social reformers who had spread liberal and progressive ideas,
the immediate motive was economic. The record of the French
Revolution therefore presents the historian with a confusing
kaleidoscope of social grievances, economic claims, generous
aspirations, literary shibboleths; and even this image is distorted by eighteenth-century terminology and by oratorical
flights of grandiloquence inherent in a period of emergency.

During the last stages of the Third Republic it became a
habit for all parties to appeal to the 'principles of the French
Revolution', although politicians were in most cases referring
to concepts which sprang up only during the industrial revolution of the nineteenth century. It had become a parliamentary
practice to invoke the ideals of 1789 on behalf of a 'proletariat',
non-existent in those days, whose equivalent in terms of class
was then allowed very few political rights. Yet once it had
sown its wild oats, the French Revolution left only a strongly

bourgeois social framework which became in the nineteenth and twentieth centuries the main bulwark of national conservatism.

The first claims which led to the setting of the revolutionary stage in France were financial. In fiscal matters the Crown was not responsible for its policy to any popular assembly. The only institution which bore any resemblance to the English Parliament was the *Etats-Généraux*. This assembly, which consisted of delegates from the clergy, the nobility, and the third-estate, could only be convened upon a summons by the king, to discuss taxation in the light of local information supplied by its members. The third-estate did not represent what is known to-day as 'the people', but only the rich citizens. In 1789, the *Etats-Généraux* had not assembled for 156 years.

The only other assemblies which could effectually modify regal absolutism were the parliaments of Paris and the provinces. They were judicial bodies which recorded, registered, and endorsed royal legislation, and in legal proceedings were entitled to question the validity of Orders in Council. In the last resort, their decrees could be annulled by the king and, on the whole, the parliament's political influence, whenever it was brought to bear upon any issue, exerted itself on behalf of interests other than the service of the common people.

The French Constitution, which was not embodied in a charter but depended on a set of laws and customs, thus possessed no safety-valve. In case of discontent, the people had no constitutional channels of self-expression. Hence the frequent resort to direct action in the form of riots or rebellions, which has marked French history and outlived the Revolution. In medieval and post-medieval times the *Etats-Généraux* had assembled periodically. From Richelieu onwards they never met. Through provincial officials and some local assemblies, the king could keep contact with the people's feelings. This, however, presupposed a degree of care and attention to which the last Bourbons hardly ever attained. National emergency almost invariably aroused popular demonstrations of allegiance on which the monarchy could depend in time of war. But anticlimax always followed in the shape of discontent which could find no lawful utterance and often turned into disaffection. The French sovereigns had relied for too long upon the element of faith in the French mental make-up and disregarded the reverse side of the French character: political criticism, nonconformity, deep-rooted possessive instinct, and hostility to taxation. When, set in this traditional context, the progress in political education stimulated a sense of social justice and of economic equity, the basic factors of constitutional revision had emerged.

Moreover, in the years which preceded the Revolution, the unpopularity of the Crown's fiscal policy increased for other reasons; throughout the century, the record of the monarchy in every field of action was not encouraging. The realm as such had not been jeopardized, but the French had paid for several wars under two reigns without observing any other results than successive losses in power and prestige. Even on ill-understood issues, such as that of the Colonies, the people sensed incompetence. At the same time, king and nobles retained tremendous financial privileges which French realism tolerated as long as they proved justified, but which it viewed with impatience when they became more and more blatantly parasitic. A French farmer might accept philosophically the making of a huge fortune by a Soubise when he considered the fact that, generation after generation, the Soubise family had one or two heads broken in the king's service. He was more reluctant to do so when the same Soubise deserted the sword for the madrigal and the battlefield for the royal antechamber. At the same time, the privileged holders of a decaying power were becoming less capable of resisting demands made upon them. Among the nobility, liberal ideas had been made fashionable by the greatest minds of the century, who behaved towards the aristocracy as Mr. Bernard Shaw behaved towards the English public, and found an audience among those very classes whom they made their target. It may be said, therefore, not only that the people's mood was ripe for political reform, but that the class at whose expense this reform was to be carried out had become morally and physically less capable of resistance.

The stage was therefore set in 1789 for economic, social, and constitutional reform. Generally speaking, such a reformation was the sole aim of the Revolution in its first stages. Privileges were a stumbling-block to economic progress. Freedom from taxation, which was extended to those classes, the nobility and the clergy, which owned the greater part of the country's wealth, had two equally disastrous effects. The first was that the State burden was borne exclusively by the people. This was not only unjust but also economically absurd, because the national revenue fell far short of its proper figure on a basis of general taxation. The second was the relatively low productivity of those parts of the realm which were protected by privilege. Moreover, economically, the kingdom was not united. Customs duties were still imposed from province to province,[1] a

[1] An odd survival of those days was still to be found during the late 1920s in the shape of customs duties on goods which entered Paris from the provinces (the 'Octroi' of Paris).

state of affairs which restricted trade and, although the duties
brought some additional revenue into the king's coffers, the
final result was a loss of income for the Treasury.

When, under popular pressure, the king consented to sum-
mon the *Etats Généraux* in 1789, fiscal revision was the main
subject to be treated. However, this Assembly in its traditional
form could not secure any serious alteration in the *status quo*,
for a simple reason: it was normally composed of representatives of the three orders, nobility, clergy, and the third-estate
in equal numbers, and the voting was not individual but by
groups. The two privileged classes were therefore bound to
secure a decision in their own favour and it could not be hoped
that they would dispossess themselves for the sake of social
improvement. From the outset the mere formulation of fiscal
grievances raised a constitutional issue: only an increase in the
numbers of the third-estate's representatives, coupled with the
institution of individual voting, could give the commons a
chance of gaining their ends. The constitutional amendment
was granted and the Assembly worked on the basis of
double representation and individual voting for the third-
estate.

The constitutional foundations had been laid for the work
of political revision. But the forces which had made for economic and social transformation could not be contained within
the framework of the Assembly. Either because the reforms
had been delayed too long, or because of temperamental dispositions inherent in the French people, or because of the
grave mistakes and even the grievous faults of the Court, most
probably by the cumulative effect of all three, two 'revolutions' took place and developed at the same time, the first
within constitutional bounds, the second in the form of direct
action by the people. It is said that, on the 14th July, 1789,
the Queen asked one of her officers to describe the scenes which
were taking place in Paris, and that he answered: 'Madam, it
is now merely a riot. But it is already growing into a revolt,
and it is likely to become a revolution.' This answer describes
the progress of the popular movement which spread outside
the precincts of the Assembly sitting in Versailles and eventually embraced the whole country.

The *Etats-Généraux* had become the *Assemblée Constituante*
and assumed executive powers, reducing the functions of the
King's ministers to pure formalities. During the same period
(1789–91) popular action kept persistently ahead of legislative
procedure. In Paris, the famous Commune, a spontaneous off-
spring of the people, soon assumed political powers. Clubs
and public meetings produced new men who went their own

way irrespective of constitutional proceedings. The Revolution was dual: with its right hand it proceeded with political revision, and with the other it wielded the new-fangled weapon of mass pressure, in the streets, in public places, even in the army and in the arsenals. Thus, when in 1791 the *Assemblée Constituante* had produced a People's Charter embodying the 'Déclaration des Droits de l'Homme', most of its work was already doomed.

'Radicals' who had sprung from the ranks of the people became the spearhead of the new Assembly: the 'Legislative'. This was France's first political parliament, a permanent institution whose purpose was not only constitutional revision, but the government of France. Its strongest elements were Republican. Their object was not only to destroy monarchic absolutism; that had been already done. They meant to destroy the monarchy altogether. The royal family played into their hands. It tried to enlist alien support and wounded French patriotism by placing dynastic interests above those of the nation. (Which was not perhaps as condemnable as it appears to us considering that, hitherto, dynastic and national interests had always been identified and the latter could hardly be conceived by traditionalists as potentially independent of the former.) When war broke out between France and those foreign powers with which the royal family had been in constant communication, the fate of the monarchy was sealed, even though the tragic end of its members was delayed.

Austria and Prussia saw in the situation a new opportunity for destroying French power in Europe. The French Assembly was unaware of the fact that the two Powers had already made an agreement. Provoked by repeated Austrian protests against the abolition of feudal rights in Alsace, and by Austrian intrigues with the French Court, it declared war on Austria in April, 1792, in the hope that Prussia and England would remain neutral. This trust in Prussia's friendliness was inherited from the philosophers of the previous era. As naïvely as Voltaire, the revolutionary leaders believed that, under the previous reign, Frederick II, the 'enlightened and liberal king', had fought against France only under pressure of circumstances: whereas Frederick had been cynically and purposely exploiting an unconscious literary Fifth Column in France.

The new King of Prussia, Frederick William II, who had fewer literary pretensions than his uncle but as many soldiers, soon undeceived the men of the Legislative Assembly. The heir to the German scheme of unification was only too ready to resume the age-old policy which for centuries French rulers

C

had kept in check. After an insolent manifesto by the Prussian General, Brunswick, Prussia attacked. But the Prussian army was stopped at Valmy.

The national emergency led to the formation of a new Assembly, the *Convention Nationale*, in which the opponents of the monarchy had the upper hand, as every new danger from abroad increased popular hostility to the royal family and to the symbol of monarchy. As an answer to the foreign challenge and to Court intrigues, the Convention proclaimed the Republic in September, 1792, and brought the King to trial. Against the imperial troops, it won the signal victory of Jemmappes. Soon, however, the Revolution's military successes led to a political miscalculation: the occupation of Antwerp, which England interpreted as a threat. The French northern frontier had been safeguarded but France was confronted with an enemy, England, who was now to fight to the bitter end: until 1815.

The year 1793 is famous in French history. The noblest sacrifices were accepted by the French nation and at the same time the greatest excesses were committed. The execution of the king and the ferocity of political repression known as 'the Terror' are partly explained by the desperate situation in which France found herself, faced on the one hand with a coalition of foreign powers, threatened on the other by political agitation of all kinds and by the royalist rebellion which followed the tragic end of Louis XVI.

Thanks to the relative unreadiness of England and to the eastern preoccupations of Prussia, Austria, and Russia, who were engaged in the criminal dismemberment of Poland, the French Republic repelled the invaders and by the end of 1793 France had been saved. The war went on, but the period of the greatest danger had come to an end.

So had the most violent phase of the Revolution. Robespierre, the symbol of the Terror, was executed. Perhaps his ruthless leadership had by its very excesses prevented internal divisions from weakening France at a crucial time. Like many historical figures, he was judged by his oppressions, and not by his achievements. One year later, Prussia and Spain concluded peace with France. The Republic had acquired the German left bank of the Rhine. Unfortunately, she had also annexed that part of Flanders which England considered, in the words of Bonaparte, as 'a loaded pistol pointing towards her heart'. Had the Republic lasted, some compromise might have been found. But the shadow of Napoleon soon began to loom over the European scene. Prussia and Austria were temporarily out of the war, England and Spain went on; Belgium remained under French control and France retained her hold over this territory until Napoleon's power was crushed by the Allies.

Meanwhile, in 1795, the reaction against the most extreme forms of the Revolution had set in. The war continued: the State was bankrupt through unbounded inflation, but the greatest external peril had passed and national life was easier. Externally and internally, tension had abated. An atmosphere of ease was spreading. The Directory (October 1795) ruled over France with gentler hands than the Convention. This relaxation at a time when French armies were still fighting on the frontiers, partly accounts for the success, popularity, and easy rise to power of Bonaparte.

In the words of Jacques Bainville, 'the Directory found in him a general who not only gained striking victories, but who made war pay instead of burdening the State's finances'. Bonaparte's Italian campaign in 1796 had resounded through France. The Revolution found pride in his lightning victories, yet he was already thinking ahead of the Revolution. Having made himself a veritable pro-consul in Italy, he took stock of his own popularity, assessed exactly the situation created by an incompetent government, and drew up the plans which he put into execution three years later in 1799 when he overthrew the Directory and paved the way for his own coronation as Emperor of the French.

Who was Bonaparte? A Corsican of French tradition and culture, a man of Italian origin educated in the eighteenth century. France, through the ages, had assimilated many men born on foreign soil. An Italian, Mazarin, had carried forward and executed the political testament of Richelieu. But this time it was a soldier, born in the island of Corsica, newly acquired in 1768, who assimilated France. Bonaparte appeared at a moment of French history when a long tradition had been broken up by the strength of a wider conception of the nation. He came at a time when France, having recanted a time-honoured faith, had not yet found her true balance and was ready to embrace a new one: the faith in the nation which Bonaparte had the supreme gift of personifying and exalting for his own ends.

Considered in retrospect, Bonaparte was and remained an extraneous body, in spite of his indebtedness to French education and mental discipline. In 1797 a French statesman in the tradition of Richelieu would have made peace even at the expense of sacrifices and unpopularity; he would have thought exclusively of the maintenance of the realm. Bonaparte's mainsprings were action and power. His genius lacked the poise of tradition and in him the adventurous instincts of a *condottiere* were not tempered by the wisdom of experience. He knew France and loved France. But he could not 'remember France'.

Bonaparte, instead of choosing the way of peace with all its temporary drawbacks in terms of national and personal prestige, chose the road to Egypt, the road to England, the road to Syria, the road which led to those coalitions which inevitably gathered around England, the road to St. Helena; he perpetuated and amplified tenfold the accidental mistake which the Revolution had made in occupying Belgium, which England throughout her history had considered as a spring-board threatening her shores. The true French political tradition would have suggested peace and the watch over Prussia on the Continent.

Some historians contend that Napoleon's main blunder was the subsequent devastation of Prussia, which is alleged to have aroused German nationalism, just as the Thirty Years War is supposed to have created it in the seventeenth century. Prussia, however, had begun her progress towards German unification and had shown her expansionist designs from the time of Frederick II. From then onwards she resumed the mission of the Habsburgs at their expense when Austria could no more hope to fulfil it. In her attempt to exploit the French Revolution, Prussia had only been frustrated in her ambitions by the superb resistance of the Republic and later by Napoleon's campaigns.

Napoleon's fundamental mistake was that he hoped to break England with an insufficient fleet; that, incapable of succeeding on the sea, he did not seek a compromise on the Belgian question but evolved instead a continental policy which must exhaust France in the end and so leave her spent, at a time when the island kingdom would threaten his western flank with intact forces; and, finally, that he further weakened Austrian power, thus 'working for the King of Prussia' and for the furtherance of the Prussian scheme of unification. Worse still, Napoleon's policy created in Europe the dangerous illusion that France was a potentially expansionist nation at the very time when she entered a 'static' era—an illusion which Germany repeatedly exploited.

England emerged from the Napoleonic wars with such tangible acquisitions as Malta, Mauritius, and other gains, and, above all, she eliminated France from Flanders. Prussia greatly increased her territories on the right bank of the Rhine.

If Prussia did not achieve more, France owed it to a diplomat of the traditional school (a diplomat who showed, incidentally, that a true sense of national interest is not always a synonym for moral sense): Talleyrand, who, at the Congress of Vienna in 1815, displayed remarkable skill in exploiting differences between the Allies. His greatest merit lay perhaps in that he clearly discerned the true interests of France in the long run. Having to take sides either with Prussia and Russia or with England and Austria, he understood that the second combination involved fewer dangers, that Prussian expansion and not England was the real threat to the existence of France. Acting on his assessment of the situation, he succeeded in limiting the effects of a Napoleonic policy which had brought France to a state of military collapse and utter physical exhaustion.

This work of salvage was the only achievement which marked the reign of the two last Bourbons, Louis XVIII and Charles X. The latter attempted to restore to the monarchy some of its former power and he was overthrown in the attempt. Yet it was not quite dead. It reappeared in its bourgeois and ultra-constitutional form with Louis-Philippe. His reign is interesting in more than one respect. It was marked by the resumption of French colonial expansion which the wars with England had checked in the eighteenth century. In the social evolution of France it witnessed a double process: an advance towards the completion of the political programme of the Revolution which had been delayed by the Napoleonic wars and the Restoration, and the parallel development of a revolutionary spirit which belonged not to the tradition of 1789 but to the age of mechanical progress, and to the birth of a new social class of industrial workers. Although the appearance and growth of that class raised a social and economic issue of the first magnitude, although it was responsible throughout the nineteenth century for a crop of collectivist dogmas (from Saint-Simon and Fourier to Marx and Engels), the problem which it set was never rationally tackled in France, not even in the twentieth century. Neither the part taken by the new class in popular demonstrations nor the warning of the Commune prevented French social evolution from developing along the old lines of 1789, with middle class and peasantry as its centre of gravity.

In foreign policy the government of Louis-Philippe tried to make a new departure: the first idea of an agreement with England took root in some French minds, despite a heavy legacy of hostility and the mark it had left upon public feeling. Three manifestations of the government's intentions in this respect are worth noting: Louis-Philippe's refusal to allow a French prince to accept the Belgian crown, which was followed by a French participation in the rise of Belgium to independence; the refusal to maintain French support of Mehmet Ali when it became obvious that this would provoke a coalition in which England would take part; the decision to close the Pritchard incident in the Pacific when France was already pursuing the conquest of Algeria. This attempted policy failed when England herself encouraged the awakening of 'nationalities' on the Continent, resuming the path which the French Revolution had followed. Prussia realized that this English policy could be exploited to her own end, the furtherance of German unity under Prussian rule and at the expense of heterogeneous Austria. Louis-Philippe decided to support Austria. This was not only the end of all hope of an agreement with England, it was also one of the causes of his downfall.

The French Revolution was still on the move; French national aspirations found an apparent correspondence in the revival of national and reformist tendencies in Germany and Austria. The French people thought in terms of ideology rather than history. At the same time, even the constitutional monarchy had become an anachronism. The revolution of 1848 overthrew Louis-Philippe. This time it was not only the *bourgeoisie* which completed the work of 1789, for Louis-Philippe's rule had been the triumph of the *bourgeoisie*. It was the coalition of intellectual, liberal, and (especially) popular elements drawn from the industrial class.

The Second Republic was proclaimed and made its first experiment in a truly universal vote. French nationalism, which had been exalted by Napoleon, and which, despite 1815, suffered from a sense of frustration, found its expression after the prudent reign of Louis-Philippe in the election of the ex-Emperor's nephew, Louis-Napoleon Bonaparte, who, like his uncle, drew his power from a revolution only to curb it and to set the clock back for twenty years. Louis-Napoleon was the champion of the 'principle of nationalities' which expressed generous tendencies and yet, when it triumphed in Germany, turned into the gravest threat to the existence of France.

It has often been said that the nephew's history was a caricature of the uncle's. Like Bonaparte, he rose to the Empire by an unconstitutional act, after two years of Presidency of the Republic. The reign shows a similar deviation from realism and the true line of French policy. Under the principle of nationalities, Napoleon III displayed in European affairs a liberalism which was lacking in his internal policy —whilst the interests of the nation demanded a rule liberal within and more conservative without. The power of Prussia was growing. By his alliance with England during the Crimean

War Napoleon made a step in the right direction. But at the Congress of Paris in 1856 his diplomacy faltered. England was satisfied once Russia had been weakened in the East. Napoleon should have pressed her, in exchange for his help in the Crimean War, to support the rebuilding of Poland as a counterpoise to Prussia. This, at least, would have been a welcome application of the principle of nationalities. He did not. France had thus alienated Russia without compensation and without reaping the benefit of an alliance with England. An agreement with Austria was on the other hand rejected, although it provided a safeguard against Prussia, because Napoleon, by virtue of the same principle, preferred to encourage national tendencies in the Austrian Empire. It was for the same reason that the Emperor led his armies into Italy to free the Peninsula 'from the Austrian yoke'. Even in this he proved inconsistent, for he abandoned the enterprise in midstream. He had succeeded in disappointing the Italians and at the same time antagonizing Austria, the only conservative force in nineteenth-century Germanism. Finally, to put the finishing touch to political incoherence, he tried to placate Austria by supporting Maximilian's claim to the Mexican throne, but when she was attacked by Prussia, he witnessed with complete indifference the crushing of the Austrian army at Sadowa in 1866 and lost the last chance of confronting Prussia with a serious coalition. Henceforth, Prussia—Germanism in its worst and most acute form—would bring all her weight to bear against the Rhine frontier and resume the path of invasion. The last means of checking her by the threat of a stronger combination had slipped through France's fingers.

The crowning result of Napoleon III's policy was the war of 1870-1, in which Bismarck gave himself the supreme luxury of saddling France with the apparent responsibility of the conflict, when in fact this great German statesman had trapped Napoleon into joining issue with Prussia under the worst conditions. Napoleon's preparations had been on a par with his diplomacy. The worst effect of the French defeat was not the annexation of Alsace-Lorraine, it was the unification of Germany under Prussian rule.

The reign of Napoleon III had been more than a caricature of that of his uncle. It had done more for Germany than the Habsburgs or Frederick the Great. Napoleon's policy had led to the rise of the power which France had kept in check for more than a thousand years.

After the collapse of the Second Empire, France resumed her march towards social and political liberalism. Once more, in 1871, the spearhead of an extreme revolutionary movement

had appeared, ahead of the normal process of evolution, the
'Commune de Paris', not only a legacy from 1789, but the
first acute manifestation of discontent among a class which had
found neither its balance nor its status, and an inspiration to
the Russian Revolution of 1917. The Commune was broken
under the eyes of the German army of occupation but left an
enduring tradition behind it. Constitutionally, the first years
of the Third Republic were marked by the last spasms of militant monarchism in France. Monarchic thinkers influenced
even the drafting of the Constitution of 1875. But the Republic
had come to stay.

The Third Republic has recently been the object of vicious
attacks. Its institutions have been accused of being responsible
for the present plight of France. Whatever happened between
1919 and 1939—and the real causes of the crisis were not
constitutional—no accusation could be more unfair and more
unjustified.

In 1875 the French Republic found an international situation which for several reasons was more unfavourable to
France than almost any in the nation's previous history.
Before the colossal power of Germany, the country was
weakened in every respect. For the first time since the beginning of the Thirty Years War, her man-power and physical
resources of all kinds were inferior to those of Germany,
whose population and industrial might were rapidly increasing.
The Second Empire had estranged every possible friend and
ally, and the First Empire's legacy of French unpopularity
survived in Europe. Faced with such odds, the Third Republic
achieved together two tremendous tasks which neither the
decaying monarchy of the eighteenth century nor the genius of
Napoleon had succeeded in carrying out: it rebuilt France's
position in Europe and gave her a vast colonial Empire.

Whilst in the eighteenth century France's colonial expansion had antagonized England, not only did the Republic conquer huge territories without damaging its relations with her
(a hope also fondly entertained by Germany), but it succeeded
in cementing a friendship with Great Britain which saved
Europe in 1914. It restored French military power as a barrier
to German expansionism.

The weight of France in the seventeenth century was not to
be regained. The inescapable fact was that, in 1914, Germany
had seventy million inhabitants and France thirty-nine million.
The counterpoise to Germany could not be found only in
military might. It had to be found in diplomacy. A foreign
policy which succeeded in that endeavour while at the same
time allowing France to conquer the second largest colonial

II. TYPES
OF
FRENCH-
MEN

1. DRINKING
WINE
(*Black Star*)

2. VILLAGE
POSTMAN
(*Black Star*)

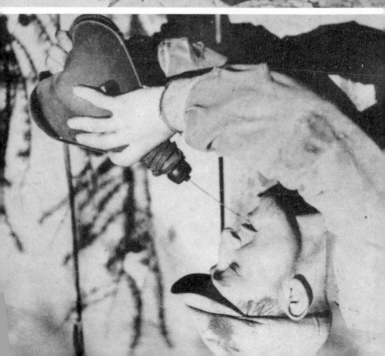

empire in the world can hardly be considered a failure. It was
in fact a great historical achievement.

With resources relatively more restricted than at any previous
time in her national life, France, under the Third Republic,
from 1875 to 1919, accomplished one of the chief objects of
her traditional policy, dictated by her situation on a continent
where she lies more exposed than any other nation: the unity
and power of the realm.

In the social field the Republic lived on the heritage of the
French Revolution and its testament of liberal and progressive
reform. When the first Great War broke out it was beginning
to tackle the new problem raised by the particular evolution
and social dynamism of the growing industrial classes. The
world conflict interrupted this process like many others, and,
in this, its effects were far-reaching.

But when in November 1918 Foch, General of the Republic,
imposed an armistice on Germany on behalf of the Allied and
Associated Powers, the Third Republic had done its duty to
France in Europe, overseas, and in the world. Indeed it had,
in its turn, served France and not only France but also European civilization as well as any régime could have done. It was
only after the first World War that its merits were questioned.
After the disaster of 1940 the constitutional problem, like most
others, must exercise French minds. Only when emotions
have calmed down and wounds have been healed can a lasting
solution be found.

CHAPTER III

THE FRENCH PEOPLE

IT is often said of man that he is a 'political animal'. In
more ways than one, this especially applies to the French.
For better or for worse, the Frenchman is a 'political
animal'. Eminently fitted to live in society, the French are at
the same time particularly susceptible to collective atmosphere.
The first quality accounts for the wide human appeal of French
culture, the second for the over-sensitiveness of the French in
political life. The French have a long national history behind
them. It has taught them the mutability of all things political
and has given them on the other hand an inborn belief in
national continuity. Régimes and governments will change,
France will go on: that conviction is axiomatic for every
Frenchman. It has its drawbacks, one of which is an occa-

sional indifference to governmental instability and even a readiness to encourage it. Indeed, the French are often inclined to consider government and administration merely as accessories after the fact—the permanent fact being France—and to treat them as temporary and superficial manifestations of the nation's life. Hence perhaps, in public affairs, the very great part played in France by high officials of the Civil Service as against politicians, the former representing the permanent factor. (Thus, in the years which preceded the last War, the Cambons had a greater influence on the foreign policy of France than the ministers under whom they served. Thus too, after that conflict, Berthelot, Secretary of the Foreign Ministry, for many years influenced foreign policy more than did any of his chiefs.) Politics as such are apt to become in France a matter for controversy rather than responsibility. An extreme and fertile diversity of political opinions and conceptions naturally favours this tendency in an imaginative community.

The French are, above all, a product of history. They are bound together by common memories, common traditions of thought, action, and behaviour, and not by ethnological or so-called racial ties. When in the last century the Comte de Gobineau evolved racialist theories in France long before Ludendorff or Hitler dreamt of putting them into practice, the consensus of French opinion was that they might be very help · ful in the breeding of horses, but would serve no purpose among civilized men whose bonds, after centuries of Christianity and culture, were of a somewhat higher quality.

But history's legacy is not only a national way of life, nor even a single national purpose. It also leaves behind it many conflicting tendencies, a variety of local traditions, a huge keyboard of political notions, beliefs, and aspirations, together with a number of prejudices. The French political picture, in the twentieth century, reflects at its best the infinite variety of the nation's past. Memories die hard in French national life. It is not irrelevant to point out that in French schools the study of history is given a much higher place than that of geography. Not many years ago, after so many wars and upheavals, it was still not uncommon to hear French peasants in the western provinces recalling the monarchist rebellions of Vendée in 1793 and clenching their fists at the 'Blues', as though this feud between Royalists and Republicans was a vivid recollection instead of an old chapter of the French tale. It might well be that in the nearest harbour a Communist docker was at the same moment rousing a café audience to fever pitch by asserting the right of the people to claim a Dictatorship of the Proletariat. Absolute and constitutional monarchy, administrative regionalism, mili-

tary and civil dictatorship, despotic and liberal popular government, and even foreign administration of their own land: the
French have known all these régimes. And, by a paradox
which is more apparent than real, the unique degree of their
national experience has made them at the same time sceptical
as to the intrinsic value of any particular form of government
and yet remarkably vehement and passionate in the expression
and manifestation of their beliefs and convictions.

It must not be forgotten that while French unity is the
most ancient in Europe, the enforcement and operation of
democratic institutions in France are comparatively recent.
The French Revolution of 1789 only completed its task some
sixty-five years ago. Once, at a dinner given on a great diplomatic occasion, the old Duke of Devonshire was sitting by a
well-known French lady who assailed him with ceaseless questions on English political problems. The old Duke was not
particularly communicative and gossip has it that he was in
the habit of lapsing into occasional slumbers between courses.
Eventually his neighbour thought that she would perhaps
draw him out by asking a really pointed question: 'I wish you
could tell me', she said, 'why democratic institutions seem to
work so much more smoothly in England than in France.'
'Madame,' he answered at last, 'the reason is quite obvious.
We cut off our own king's head a hundred and forty-four
years before you did yours,' and then he dozed again.

Democracy as a form of government is a recent institution
which has been dearly bought. The sense and enjoyment of
rights finally conquered are therefore stronger in the French
political make-up than the consciousness of collective responsibility. The French feel a strong allegiance and duty to the
nation as a fatherland which must be protected and perpetuated,
and a far weaker obligation towards the State and its representatives. This is partly a survival from those days when the
only link between the State and the individual members
of the nation was the tax-collector. There is a saying that
'The French carry their hearts on the left and their wallets
on the right.' Transcribed into political language, it means
that the French are ready to give their lives for their country,
but not their money to the government.

What is often lacking in French public life is the sense of
moral responsibility and of individual contribution to the community. Fundamentally, the French are perhaps the most
democratically minded people in the world, not only in their
unrivalled love of freedom but in their indifference to social
distinctions. Whatever snobbery there may be in France is
quite independent of social hierarchy. A young man may

preen himself at having lunched with Giraudoux, or Derain, or even with a famous political agitator, but very few would boast of having met anybody who mattered on purely social grounds. Religious, social, moral, racial tolerance pervades every branch of French life and every French community. It is only in time of crisis, and then only to a limited extent, that signs of intolerance may appear in common life.

Yet this deeply democratic instinct, when applied to politics and to government, proves a less active force than in daily life, for it is truly an instinct which influences the French way of living, far more than a mental discipline trained and practised in the control of public affairs and in the exercise of public administration, as it is in England through a long-standing parliamentary tradition.

Like most other human dispositions, French individualism is both an asset and a liability. It encourages vigilance in the protection of freedom, tolerance, and most human rights. On the other hand, it often blurs what would normally be a clear vision of the general interest, when this interest is not emphasized by an actual national emergency. Daily sacrifices to the State in the form of money or services are probably more difficult for a French citizen than for an Englishman, a Dutchman, or a Swede.

The specific character and motive of French individualism are not always properly understood. The Frenchman's attitude to State problems originates not merely in his ancestors' reactions of self-defence to despotic power. It has even deeper roots in Christian tradition. According to this, the basic social cell is the family, and the first individual duty consists in its protection, welfare, and prosperity. In spite of current prejudices the patriarchal sense is far stronger in France than in most other countries. It even found its political expression in the persistent refusal of very democratic parliaments to grant women the right to vote. It is coupled in France with a congenital attachment to private property. The acquisition and retention of property, and preferably land, is not only the aim of every French peasant: it is the unavowed dream of many an industrial worker even if on his factory's platform he champions the final abolition of all rights of ownership. The link in the French mind between the family instinct and the possessive one is evidenced by the persistence in the twentieth century of the practice of providing brides with dowries. Finding a concrete, tangible, and secure basis for family life has always been one of the great French preoccupations. The family, like the State, must have its finances, its stability, its future, and, if possible, its domain. This similarity itself creates a

fundamental antagonism between the respective claims upon
the individual of the family and of the State. 'I would rather
give it to my children than to the government'—is a phrase
which might be heard time and again in the French provinces
as an expression of discontent, or simply as outlet for grum-
bling away some grudge against the local council.

In the last century, Balzac described in his novels the
dramatic ferocity to which the service of family interests
could drive its responsible members, while in almost every one
of his plays Labiche ridiculed the hagglings of French parents
over dowry and financial position.

The world painted in sombre or in light colours by Balzac
and Labiche is no more. But the old struggle, family versus
State, has left enduring marks on French individualism. In the
twentieth century they were still very apparent among the
peasantry and the provincial *bourgeoisie*, a combination which
amounts to more than half of the French population. It is
by no means certain that they were not part of the mental
framework of classes whose passage from rural to industrial
conditions was still comparatively recent.

The social conceptions, behaviour, aspirations, and claims
of rural and of industrial France are naturally profoundly different. In this respect (and apart from any modern dogmas)
there is in France a fundamental dualism. On this specifically
French phenomenon, Mr. Thomas Kernan, in his book, *Report
on France*, makes some observations which deserve to be
quoted: 'If I were constrained to describe it [this dualism] in
a phrase I would use the title of Stendhal's novel, *The Red and
the Black*. The red personality of France may be said to be
progressive, revolutionary, anti-clerical, Jacobin, romantic in
the Rousseau sense, democratic with hope in man equal to its
faith in God. The black personality is conservative, orderly,
Catholic, classic, aristocratic, Latin. In politics, economics,
education, and culture the two aspects of Janus-faced France
are opposed. What is more, it would be difficult to explain the
division on a strictly class basis. The conservative tradition
may be maintained by the poorest village peasant, while many
of the wealthy industrialists would certainly place themselves
on the Jacobin side. The separation perhaps goes deeper than
class into the psychological past of the individual. The Conservatives are oriented towards the provinces, away from
Paris. They are regionalists while the Jacobin-Liberals are
centralists. The Conservatives are agrarians in the main. The
Jacobins are apt to think in terms of an industrial France,
and, rich and poor alike, their centre is the mill and its problems. The demand of the blacks is for more discipline, order,

duty; the traditional slogan of the reds is "liberty, fraternity, equality".'

There is perhaps in this intelligent analysis too clean a classification. Perhaps some of its features might justify re-touching: the 'Latin' character of the 'blacks' is somewhat dubious when one remembers that the strongly Catholic and traditionally conservative elements in France were drawn from such typically Celtic regions as the west and south of Brittany. And if 'the demand of the blacks is for more discipline', this is more true in individual and local life than it is in public national life, if one understands by 'discipline' the acceptance of a collective code enforced by the State at the expense of the individual and of the family's interests. Nevertheless, Mr. Kernan's picture remains in its essentials a very valuable assessment of two conflicting elements in the French political formation.

The part played in French history by faith is generally underestimated, although it accounts for the acceptance of absolute monarchy long after that method of government had ceased to justify its existence. In politics, the French have for centuries been far nearer to the Christian conception than to the Greek (or to the basic English conception), far more in-clined to faith than to moral responsibility. Even the great Revolution did not destroy this aptitude for faith, but only transformed it. When in 1791 the Baltic revolutionary leader, Anacharsis Clootz, cried to the French, 'O France, guéris-toi des individus', he was warning them against their tendency to pin their faith to symbolic men: symbolic, under the monarchy, of a Divine Right, symbolic afterwards of the Nation's great-ness. It is a remarkable fact that ten years after a revolution which founded its political reforms on moral and collective responsibilities rather than on belief, the whole French people rose to the appeal of a legendary individual and followed in his wake for nearly twenty years, until France was almost bled to death.

A passage from a book published in unoccupied France in 1941 (*France d'hier, France de demain*) by Jean Pupier, very clearly sums up the historical process resulting from this funda-mental tendency of the French character: 'This people of believers, the French, has been prodigal of its faith. It has placed it in its religion, in its nobles, in its monarchy, and eventually, despairing of them all, in itself. Now and then, it has given it to a few outstanding men. In each of these suc-cessive phases, it stubbornly persevered, often beyond reason-able hope. But the most dearly paid disappointments are also the deepest.'

In nations as in individuals the reaction to disillusioned faith is not always despair or revolt. In the French people it has never been despair and not always rebellion. They have often sought refuge and utterance in a mental attitude, a form of scepticism, or even political cynicism. Those who see effects without examining their causes are inclined to describe the French as sceptical, 'Voltairian', systematically nonconformist in politics; in a word, they are apt to mistake a reaction of self-defence for a fundamental disposition. The truth is that, although they developed at successive stages, the two elements are ever present. Even in recent years, the comparative ease with which common political agitators could enlist the sincere support of French groups merely by appealing to an ancient yearning for belief, enthusiasm, and even sacrifice, has baffled many students of French political life. Once undeceived, the French are all the more ready to jump to the other extremes of disaffection and intellectual criticism or cynicism, for which their mind is well prepared and equipped.

An example of callousness resulting from utter loss of faith in every political creed may be found in the story of an old gentleman of the last century, the father of the painter Degas, a monarchist by conviction, who had been disgusted with the bourgeois domination of the Louis-Philippe régime and yet disliked even more the revolution which overthrew it. During the worst days of 1848, he was watching, with the contempt of an expert, one of the improvised soldiers of the revolution wasting bullet after bullet in a vain attempt to shoot a Garde National at a hundred yards. At last, exasperated by the fellow's clumsiness, he went up to him and said: 'Come on, my friend, give me that rifle. I'll show you how to shoot.' And almost without taking aim, he shot the Garde National through the head. 'My God,' said the rioter, respectfully, 'you had better keep that rifle. You will get a few more of these rascals!' 'I can't oblige,' replied the old gentleman, handing back the gun, 'I am afraid I don't share your opinions.' Nothing short of a foreign invasion would have aroused any exaltation in that old political atheist.

Confronted with such a national emergency, 'blacks' and 'reds', or even 'blasés' (which should be added to Mr. Kernan's categories as an important by-product of both trends) become immediately conscious of a common denominator: France. The revolutionary tradition of the 'Rush to the Frontiers' and the peasant's attachment to his land converge towards the same end. One of the most striking phenomena in the history of France was the remarkable acceptance of conscription by the French at a time (1792) when such a demand had never been made upon any people.

A Frenchman may display indifference or cynicism in capital economic issues such as his country's budget; he may even entertain subversive opinions on most State matters, or openly antagonize every conceivable form of régime or government and abuse them all to his heart's content: all these are not commonly considered as breaches of the individual code of honour. But the breach is recognized and condemned as such when the same attitude is taken towards a threat against the nation's existence. Lack of national spirit in that case is not condoned or even tolerated, but held as a violation of the most natural and fundamental laws. Not only is conscientious objection rejected by French society as an extenuating circumstance, but it is regarded as an aggravating one. Lack of spirit might be forgiven as a human failing; not so a deliberate refusal to share in a common sacrifice.

With very few exceptions, Internationalism among French political groups is more intellectual than real. In a little sketch at the Palais Royal a few years ago, the review artist Rip gave an amusing example of the triumph of instinctive patriotism over doctrinal catechism. Two plumbers are working on a roof. One of them, a Communist, is scoffing at his mate's old-fashioned notions of patriotism and calls the flag 'an old rag'. Presently they hear the first bars of the National Anthem. A regiment is marching by below. The mate looks over and stands to attention. The other watches him ironically. Then, almost unconsciously, as the stirring strains of the 'Marseillaise' sound nearer and nearer, he stretches himself up, and at last as the flag passes before his eyes, he mechanically takes off his cap. Gradually the music dies away. 'Well,' says his companion, 'so you did salute the silly rag.' But by then the other has returned to his theories. 'What, I?' he says. 'Salute *that*? Don't be a fool—only, you see, a chap in the colour escort happens to be a pal of mine.'

Of all the issues confronting the individual in a community, national emergency is the only one which invariably provokes an identical reaction. The sense of national peril and of national service when it arises is inborn and hereditary. By tradition, it is *the* essential collective duty: the only general interest which every individual Frenchman considers with unqualified seriousness of purpose.

Nor is this seriousness merely accidental in the French character and in French life. It is, on the contrary, one of their fundamental features. In his work, on his land, in family problems, a Frenchman shows an uncommon seriousness and

D

even intensity of purpose. The earnestness of a reaper at his task, from dawn to dusk, the gravity of any discussion even on matters of daily routine by the members of a French family, the extreme care exercised in the choosing of a profession by a young Frenchman even if he is beginning as an apprentice, and even such familiar scenes as a French mechanic examining an engine or a clockmaker scrutinizing a watch, all these testify to the seriousness and reflection which a Frenchman applies to activities within his individual orbit. In these, there are few nations which have a deeper consciousness of the solemnity of life.

To the consideration of collective issues, according to their importance and to particular circumstances, the French apply their faith, their passion, their intelligence, or their wits. Moral responsibility and seriousness of purpose are reserved for individual and especially family pursuits. Religion has, if anything, encouraged that tendency. On the national stage, the Church has ceased to play a political part. Its national role proceeds from the cumulative effect of individual and personal influences. These limitations placed upon the action of the Church encourage its traditional inclination to lay stress on those human interests which relate to the individual rather than to the State. Politically the Church stands half-way between strict individualism and excessive State interference. As against both, it accords its wholehearted support to the family. To that extent, it is a factor of resistance to the natural process of centralization.

The contrast in the French character between two mental attitudes, one to problems of general interest and the other to matters which remain within the compass of the individual, is another aspect of 'the French dualism'. Vehemence and oratorical fervour may be the keynotes of a café controversy on the choice of a member for parliament. When it comes to marrying the elder daughter or even deciding whether the family's land should be increased by a few acres of pasture, there is less heat in argument and far more deliberation in the choice. The contrast is somewhat less marked among the labouring classes and, generally speaking, among those sections of the population whose existence is not directly associated with the land. But still it exists. A French workman is more conservative in his habits than in his political opinions. The latter may change more readily than his painfully furnished cottage, if he has one. His domestic authority is of greater moment to him than even the gain of two or three seats in parliament for his party. And he himself may show passion in political debates but will certainly prefer to use reflection at home. The difference between the industrial classes and the peasantry lies not so much in the relative importance attached by both to individual as against collective preoccupations, as in their conflicting views on collective problems considered in themselves. In these, the industrial classes display more idealism, more belief in wide human solutions by general co-operation, and also more combative ardour when their hopes are frustrated; the peasantry is more realistic, more patient, more sceptical towards comprehensive and sweeping reforms, more resigned to its fate when disappointment comes. The former is apt to believe that if a new order of things arises, his own condition and that of his family will improve in body and soul; the latter would incline to the view that these great changes might impair a hard-won equilibrium and encroach upon its patrimony.

Their political interests are divergent and often conflicting. Their modes of expression, social reactions, and even conceptions of community life are almost contradictory. Yet their most profound aspirations are not dissimilar. These reveal themselves in domestic pursuits, in which, despite the lighter aspects of French life which give rise to many prejudices, the essential tendencies of the French are towards order, security, and continuity. In that sense, the French are individually conservative and classical. The problem of applying individual qualities to the service of the nation is of course one of the main contemporary issues in all States. It is certainly vital in France. In fact, it has already proved so in the twentieth century.

From almost every hilltop in France one can look down upon a vast mosaic of neatly cut fields on which men are bending to till and to reap, and have been so bending for countless generations; in the distance the spire of a church rises above the tile or slate roofs of some orderly town, perhaps on the banks of a river. Usually, the factory stands on the extreme edge; further still is a line of other fields; and, much beyond, one can imagine Paris, where life never stops. In the fields, in the provincial towns, in the factory, in the capital, Frenchmen are working or resting. Their expectations, their ambitions, their demands, are moderate. They have a deep-rooted sense of measure and of reality. By tradition they know the art of living and of balanced economy. They occasionally haggle over money, which is a symbol of patient effort, and yet in many wars they have given their blood without complaining. They have fought among themselves on religious, political, social, and even ethical issues (such as the guilt or innocence of some particular man), and yet they have given supreme examples of national unity. They are, on the whole, sedentary and conservative, but they have often left their comfortable homes to die in foreign lands for the independence of peoples whom they hardly knew—in Poland, in Greece, in Italy, in America, and elsewhere. They praise order above all in their houses, and persistently question it in their State. They are believers, and they have endowed European thought with its greatest traditions of intellectual criticism. An enumeration of apparent contrasts does not amount to an analysis: it may, at best, be a warning against any attempt to sum up with finality the character of a nation.

CHAPTER IV

THE FRENCH MIND AND FRENCH CULTURE

VARIETY of temperament and deep contrasts between individual dispositions may occasionally become national liabilities in point of political power. In the realm of thought and culture diversity remains an unqualified asset. The very differences in aspirations, moods, beliefs which have marked French history as well as those which proceed from geographical diversity have been responsible for the wealth of France in cultural accomplishment. At the junction of most European currents of thought and artistic inspiration France partook of every influence, received and gave without counting. In addition to her own natural versatility, she has caught the successive reflections of European civilization and thereby put new touches to the French picture, enlivening it with fresh colouring.

Yet in its infinite diversity, the French contribution is clearly and constantly recognizable. What is it that makes a French book, a French painting, a French monument, identifiable as such? For a landscape by Corot, independently of its subject, could no more have been painted outside France than the theme of Ibsen's *Master Builder* could have been conceived outside Scandinavia. And what is it that renders any French literary or artistic achievement essentially 'communicable', easily assimilable by other nations? With very few exceptions these qualities have been persistently present throughout the cultural history of France, and have made her the cultural clearing-house of Europe. Many partial definitions of the French mind have been given, often in the shape of epigrams or generalizations such as: 'The French are a

III. AMIENS CATHEDRAL

nation of Moralists'—'The French are a nation of Painters'—
'The French are a nation of Novelists'. Such propositions
merely beg the question. They single out a particular form of
expression as distinctive of the French in order to suggest a
set of gifts which are left undescribed.

Any attempt to define national characteristics comprehen-
sively is always presumptuous and generally futile. It may be
of more value to record those qualities which are constant
enough in the French mental make-up to be accepted as
'dominant', and to trace their manifestation in the French
cultural heritage.

The most highly developed sense in the French is probably
their gift of sight. Physically and morally their most permanent
attribute is clearsightedness, clarity, and lucidity of vision.
To see 'things as they are' is the great French preoccupation.
Neither religious fervour nor flights of mysticism can noticeably impair this fundamental aptitude; they merely transpose
it to a different plane. The quality and power of the eye are
to the French the basic means of investigation—to such an
extent that Romanticism in France marked a departure from
literary tradition mainly in its pursuit of 'colourfulness' and
visual evocation, as against German Romanticism, for instance,
which admittedly was richer in thought.

Exponents of Determinism would ascribe this disposition to
the influence of a climate in which neither mist nor the excessive blaze of the sun affects clarity or true perspective. Whatever the explanation may be, this gift is undoubtedly responsible not only for the greatness of French painting but also for
the mental attitude of the French to ethical problems and to
most human issues. Their approach is naturally realistic. To
assess, to measure, to analyse, rather than to imagine, suggest,
or embellish: these are the primary aims of French artists and
even of French moralists. Indeed, Montaigne, the pioneer in
mental scrutiny (at least among the lay-writers), made a special
point of not endeavouring to reconcile those contradictions
which he detected in himself and which he accepted as attributes of humanity. Imagination is traditionally recognized as
a prerequisite to creation, but the French are inclined to regard
it as indispensable raw material without which nothing can be
done, but which is of little value in itself if it is not disciplined.
So great a Christian thinker as Pascal not only rejected it, even
as a mystical stimulus, but condemned it as 'the engineer of
errors and falsehoods'.

Faith itself, in the truly French cultural tradition, is not
divorced from realism and temporal clearsightedness. It does
not blur the outline of the human image, nor does it attempt

to idealize it. In fact, throughout French history the only instance of a lasting breach with fundamental realism as a means of investigation was the school of Rousseau, whose study of human problems proceeded from philosophic assertions such as 'the Native Goodness of Man', in direct contradiction to orthodox religious thought.

The exact knowledge and presentation of man is thus the persistent object of French artistic creation. It might be said that the French, even in ethics, are moral commentators rather than reformers. The Revolution and the movements which originated in it have altered this tradition in the field of sociology and politics, but in the realm of culture the effect has not endured. Even such contemporary schools as the 'Populistes', have distinguished themselves by accurate descriptions of atmosphere more than by literary efforts in social reform.

These qualities of true vision, of realism, and of precision in analysis and description, carry with them a deep-rooted hostility to any form of confusion in thought and expression. The French like to see men as they are. A systematically idealized version of a human character may well be to the French observer as much of a monster as a Frankenstein to a cinema audience. Reality is equally distant from both. And if the French have often produced in fiction characters of such perfect beauty as Madame de Mortsauf in Balzac's *Lys dans la Vallée*, it was mainly with a view to making the true nature of human shortcomings even clearer against such a background.

Of their media of expression, the French demand that they should be exactly adapted to their object. A French painter, in front of his canvas, does not attempt to be a philosopher or a poet. A French architect thinks in terms of habitation and of its relation to man, and not in terms of spectacular impressions on a sightseer. A classical French writer adapts his 'pictorial' description to the exact part which it has to play in the development of his character. Save for the romantic schools, Nature has been an object of literary study only in so far as it had a bearing upon the development of a human case. But, traditionally, the French are as precise in the use of a medium of expression and of its adaptation to the subject as they are in their process of mental investigation. In all creative activities their taste for order and discipline and their aversion to confusion between notions and means of expression are constant features of French cultural history. For example, if symbolism has been a failure in French art, it is chiefly because it used painting, a medium of visual representation, as an interpreter of ideas. In this, the French tradition proves to be as basically

different from the German as it is in political, social, and ethical
conceptions.

Discrimination is not only exercised in an exact correspondence between the object of a study and the means of inter-
preting it. One of the traditional principles in French art and
literature is the maintenance of strict objectivity, by which is
meant that the personal emotion of the artist must not invade
the realm of its creation. This may sound axiomatic in every
country. What is perhaps characteristic of the French is that
even in poetry, an essentially subjective realm, many French
schools should have enforced this principle of objectivity. Paul
Valéry, who wrote in *Littérature* that 'nothing is farther from
the state of reverie than the poet's inspiration', maintained that
it must be a supreme process of clear focusing and lucid concentration. Even a visionary poet like Rimbaud, the personification of subjectiveness in creation, still partakes of the French
visual tradition; for it is in the realm of the eyes that he finally
transcribes the aspirations of his unruly and mystical mind.
In painting, the most perfect product of visual objectivity is of
course the French Impressionist School.

Moralists, essayists, novelists, poets, painters, sculptors, and
architects have for centuries retained those specific qualities
which originate in the basic gift of clearsightedness: sense of
proportion, measure, sound diagnosis. The product of those,
as a distinctive feature of French culture, is an intellectual and
artistic civilization which is exactly to the scale of man, exactly
commensurable with man. This is as far as one may safely go
in an attempt to define the French 'mental equipment'.

Historically, for purposes of convenience, the evolution of
French culture and of French civilization could be divided
into six main phases: the Middle Ages, the Renaissance, the
Classical Age (seventeenth century), the Encyclopedists, the
Romantic Period, and, finally, the Post-Romantic phase (with
its various reactions against Romanticism) up to the first World
War. This, of course, is an entirely arbitrary classification.

Contrary to a common prejudice, the medieval era has
played a very great part in the making of French civilization.
After the partition of Charlemagne's empire, after the chaos of
the tenth century and the years of feudal anarchy which followed it, three centuries elapsed before the storm of the Hundred Years War, during which a French society established its
own foundations, evolved a modern language, an individual
mode of life, and a specific cultural tradition. Retrospectively,
these memories are often blurred by other recollections which
shock our contemporary conceptions, such as feudal servitude

(the extent of which has been grossly exaggerated) and religious despotism (which may have been one of the only means available at the time of cementing a very loose social order). Moreover, it is often assumed that cultural influences could never reach the mass of the people.

In view of such prejudices one might wonder how it is that from such dark ages a school of architecture should have been born which has been unsurpassed in French history; that the French language should gradually have reached the degree of perfection to which the last medieval chronicler, Philippes de Commines, testifies by his works, after Villehardouin, Joinville, and others; that above all it should have produced a purely French poetic tradition and metre beginning with Théroulde, the bard of the *Chanson de Roland* in the eleventh century, and finding its greatest interpreter during the reign of Louis XI in François Villon, one of the purest poets in the French language, whose use of the decametric harmony has yet to be surpassed.

When such master-builders as Robert de Luzarches and Thomas and Renaud de Cormont worked over a period of several decades on a cathedral, when enterprising minds such as Suger or Maurice de Sully devoted years of their lives to the study of new plans and their execution, when thousands of artisans and masons swarmed on slowly rising scaffolds for generations, it is difficult to assert that art was more withdrawn from the people than it is to-day. Popularization of the written word was naturally impossible before the invention of the printing press, but oral tradition afforded some means of communication, through which not only poems but also miracle-plays and farces were accessible, at least to burghers and town folk. It is perhaps a sad reflection on intellectual progress that after centuries of civilization the contemporary radio-listener should abandon study and return, out of choice, to habits developed in medieval times under the force of circumstances.

One of the clearest manifestations of a French medieval culture is the birth of an original French tradition in painting. Not only do the frescoes of Montmorillon bear witness to an early French art at the end of the twelfth century, but in the second part of the fourteenth century a real School (or at least what Mr. Clive Bell calls a clearing-house for multifarious tendencies) appeared at the Court of the first Valois. Although the most violent episodes of the Hundred Years War set the clock back, there emerge from the French provinces of Touraine, Bourbonnais, Avignonnais, such shining names as those of Jean Fouquet, Charonton, and the Masters of Moulins and

Avignon, towards the middle of the fifteenth century. These are truly great French painters. They are also the last messengers of medieval France.

The transfer of the Holy See to Avignon for seventy-six years, until 1378, and later the development of trade between France and Italy encouraged by Louis XI had introduced Italian influences. But the most powerful Italian current was not felt in France until the first part of the sixteenth century, which marks the beginning of the so-called French Renaissance and follows the expeditions of Louis XII and Francis I into Italy.

It can hardly be asserted that in art the Renaissance produced a specifically French school of painting, for the Italian touch is always noticeable. In architecture the famous castles certainly bore the marks of a strong Italian influence. But in thought and literary achievement the sixteenth century in France brought a decisive contribution to European culture and ethics, for it opened with Rabelais and closed with Montaigne, giant figures towering above the Italianate poets and writers who adorned the reigns of the last Valois.

The poets of the 'Pléiade'—Ronsard, Du Bellay, and even the more genuinely French Remy Belleau—find the true 'ring' only when they wander away from the tracks trodden by their Latin guides. But Rabelais is the flaming herald of a distinctively French Renaissance, the great father of a robust, vivid, clear-sighted, critical, tolerant, and independent literary posterity which has a realistic vision of life and yet keeps faith in it, loves it without being its dupe, seeks truth without bitterness, and denounces injustice without envy. In the face of kings, feudal magnates, and magistrates, he asserts man's freedom to look about him, to think, to judge, to question, to laugh at his own shackles, to deride prejudices and mock sectarianism, and, in the words of Laurent Tailhade, 'his giant burst of human laughter echoes through all Europe'. His is not a dogmatic, political, or religious Reformation. True to the French mind he stays within his own realm and uses his own medium. It is an assertion of individual thought and independence through thought, rising above time, régime, and circumstances. It is indeed one of the great recurrent self-affirmations of the human person in the midst of invading dogmatism, one of the great manifestations of the individual and direct approach to life and its values.

Some forty years after the apparition of Gargantua and Pantagruel, Montaigne's *Essais* endowed Europe with an even greater monument of independent thought and of human scrutiny breaking away from every ethical convention. Montaigne in his methods is perhaps in literature the equivalent of the Impressionists in painting. His lucid, penetrating eye is self-trained, his vision free from the prejudices of schools and accepted bases for study. He is in constant, direct contact with himself and with man, analysing both with the dispassionate diagnosis of a scientist bending over his subject. He knows 'how to look' and refuses to draw conclusions which it is not the privilege of man to define. He sees, states, and communicates in admirable language of which the clarity is an art in itself. His and Rabelais's are truly 'French' contributions to the progress towards knowledge of Man.

After the last legacies from the Religious Wars had been disposed of, France entered her Classical Age, the seventeenth century. Its first efforts represented by a systematic reaction against the Italianate period produced a heavy and uneasy mode of expression, a sort of moralism in poetry which, from d'Aubigné to Malherbe, makes French literature seem like a transcription from Calvinism into style. And then with the first Corneillean flourish there begins the Great Era, so rich, so bountiful, that any accurate assessment of its contribution is impossible.

This epoch, the century of Louis XIV, has its guide: Descartes, creator of a method of investigation using in its approach to human problems the sole power of the intellect as against postulates originating in theological or ethical tradition. Man, face to face with himself, not only applies to the understanding of his problems his own means of perception but evolves a method of work, of 'rational' analysis.

Throughout the Classical Age the fundamental object of philosophy, literature, and art remains the study of Man, of his nature, of his passions, of his motives, of his social habits and oddities: man as an individual to whom the existing social order provides only an artistic background, and not man against an existing order, for there is no sign of political reformism amongst its writers. Political and hierarchical foundations are accepted. Indeed this social conformity also has its drawbacks, for it is carried to the point of ignoring the rich popular vein from which medieval and pre-Renaissance art had drawn its robustness. On the other hand that conformity allows the seventeenth century to work deeply and unerringly. It is within their boundaries that the individual character offers itself as a subject to the philosopher, the poet, the painter, or the satirist. And because of this very limitation, because there is no confusion between the realms of art and politics or between aesthetic, moral, and political values, the mediums of expression are as clear, concise, and balanced as the thought.

Neither the weight of traditions and patterns borrowed from antiquity, nor the compliance with the demands of Court and aristocracy, are able to blur the clarity of vision or to overload the elegant perfection of the style. Here is true French craftsmanship in conception and interpretation: the artist looks shrewdly and exclusively at his model—whether he be Nicolas Poussin or Racine, whether he be La Bruyère, the moralist, or Bossuet, the Catholic preacher.

Even Blaise Pascal, tormented by a conflict between his yearning for blind faith and his mental power of criticism (a fundamentally French contradiction although it seldom assumed such an acute form), presented a supreme demonstration of lucidity in his very suffering. Two centuries later a similar example was given by Proust, revising in the throes of his own agony his original description of his grandmother's death (*Le Côté de Guermantes*) in the light of his own physical experience: a striking instance of clearsightedness to the last moment.

Such was the influence of the Classical Age on French literature, that its standards of expression at their best (that is, when mannerisms have been cast aside) have endured to this day and survived in their entirety. This classical style was a strong framework never broken nor distorted by the onslaught of personal emotions. Indeed, the emotional value of Racine or Molière lies precisely in the exceptional density of the expression. Passion is never exuberant and gains in intensity through measured and controlled statement. In the treatment of the subject itself, the development of the action in a play by Molière or the handling of a contemporary character by Saint-Simon remains in the twentieth century an undisputed criterion.

To assess the part played in French and European culture by the eighteenth century is no easy matter. Literature persistently trespasses on the realm of philosophy, and philosophy or the essay on the field of sociology and economics. This interdependence of pursuits and values distinguished the pre-Romantic era which coincides with the pre-Revolutionary period in politics. The ethical revolution in the eighteenth century is not less important than its social counterpart.

In the analysis of this epoch of French culture, it is sometimes difficult to avoid a confusion of issues. It is, for instance, generally held that the Encyclopedists are conjointly responsible for an intellectual revolution which inspired or at least impregnated the great social changes of 1789 and after. This is due to the physical fact that Voltaire, Rousseau, d'Alembert, Montesquieu, Diderot, and others, all worked

together in the production of the first comprehensive Ency-
clopedia, a collaboration which naturally led to a close inter-
change of ideas. However, despite the influence which they
exercised upon their time, neither Montesquieu nor even Voltaire may be considered as the real engineer of an ethical
revolution. For all their boldness, they were but classical
reformers, Montesquieu with a definite conservative leaning,
Voltaire in a more actively progressive way. The true revolutionary was Rousseau, because his social and literary philosophy
broke away from every French tradition, either intellectual or
spiritual, on absolutely fundamental principles, and not on
contingent and circumstantial factors of social evolution.

Most of the Encyclopedists of the eighteenth century belong
in literature and ethics to the individualistic tradition of Montaigne; in their approach to the human character they still live
in the Classical Age; in style they are not far removed from it;
in social philosophy they are either reformists or simply non-
conformists. Their aspirations are progressive, not revolutionary. Voltaire steps into the public arena to defend the
Protestant Calas against an alleged miscarriage of justice, and
the rights of the individual against the State. He exposes,
with scathing irony, the vanity of international wars in *Candide*, and derides most collective institutions in his philosophical short stories. But he is a profound sceptic. He does not
defend the individual out of a genuine belief in human nature.
He is, on the whole, ready to accept reforms and progress on
existing foundations. This advocate of social justice admired
an 'enlightened autocrat', Frederick II of Prussia; this caustic
historian praised the century of Louis XIV. Voltaire was above
all a disgruntled classicist whose colossal mind understood the
weaknesses of a social organization whose intellectual pro-
testantism asserted the need for amendments, corrections,
redress of wrongs. But he also possessed an inborn scepticism
which guarded him against the 'mysticism' of transformations and the belief that the greater the change, the greater
the human progress. Nor can Montesquieu, for all the monuments of learning and luminous intelligence which he left to
the Revolution, be truly held a revolutionary promoter.

With such outstanding exceptions as Beaumarchais, a veritable heir to Molière, and Chamfort, a moralist in the best
French vein, the authors of the time were dwarfed by the
philosophic writers. The Encyclopedists towered above novelists, poets, essayists, playwrights, as Montaigne had towered
in the sixteenth century above the graceful poets of the Pléiade.
Playwrights and novelists lived perfectly happily within the
precincts of this world of epigrams, of fashions bounded by

elegance, of ornate lightness, which was always within calling distance of one of the royal country houses.

The same differences in stature appear in art. There is as little in common between the Masters of one of France's greatest ages of painting and some of their fashionable contemporaries, as between Voltaire's contribution to world-thought and the delicate emotions of Marivaux's characters. Watteau and Chardin stand above their century; Fragonard, Greuze, and Boucher himself are well within it. In Chardin, France found a painter who remained absolutely true to his proper medium of expression and yet could almost be claimed as a social pioneer: for he discovered the artistic potentialities of daily life and he surprised beauty where it is least conspicuous. In music, Couperin added lustre to the years of the Regency and Rameau to the last phase of the reign of Louis XV.

Finally, for the first time, scientific philosophy produced in France an exponent whose influence was considerable in eighteenth-century Europe: Condillac, whose *Traité des Sensations* has stood the test of time.

In French culture, irrespective of their relative greatness, most of the philosophers, essayists, writers, and artists of the time belong to their century. It is not as between the genius of Voltaire and the graces of Marivaux, nor between the visual splendour of Watteau and Lancret's stage pieces, that the eighteenth century can be divided. The great breach in tradition, the true promoter of revolution, is Jean-Jacques Rousseau; with him and under his influence, the romantic period is ushered in. Whether for this reason he is greater than his contemporaries must be left as a very debatable point. The fact is that Rousseau's impact upon his century and upon European thought was decisive.

Rousseau is usually associated with the critical intellectual tradition. For chronological reasons his name is linked with that of Voltaire, his outlook likened to that of such thinkers as Montaigne in France, or Francis Bacon in England. Nothing is farther from the truth. First and foremost, Rousseau is a mystic and a believer. He is a mystic towards Nature and a believer in man. But his mental process is not criticism or scepticism; his method of approach and investigation is not independent, scientific, analytical, like those of Montaigne and Bacon. He proceeds by postulates, axioms, absolute beliefs, in exactly the same way as the orthodox theologians and exponents of scholasticism. The only difference is that his own postulates and axioms are not to be found in revelation, and that his theology is human instead of divine. His assertions of the fundamental goodness of man and of the purifying effect

of Nature on him are, according to the standards of rational
criticism, as unwarranted by objective evidence as Gospel
truths. They appertain to Faith. Socially, Rousseau is a revolutionary and an innovator. Intellectually, he could almost be
called a reactionary in the strictest sense of the term.

Rousseau's social conceptions soon depreciated, but his influence, all the same, has been enormous. It is clear that his
conviction that man was fundamentally virtuous and well-
meaning leads to an endemic feud between the individual and
society, not society at any particular time, but society as such.
For social order can never be perfect and therefore men's
individual grievances against all forms of social order will eter-
nally be justified on the bases of the Rousseauist articles of
faith. And, in fact, when Rousseau's doctrines had ceased to
have currency in France, the true heirs to his teachings were
the orthodox anarchists. The traces of his human dogmatism
are quite manifest in the works of Kropotkin.

If his social ideology as expressed in the *Contrat Social* or
Émile has not endured except as a matter for speculative discussion, his ethical outlook impressed French literature and
poetry for more than three-quarters of a century. Nature,
in Rousseau's view, provided a test of character. Man in
Nature was himself, uncorrupted by social circumstances. He
was there in his true condition. His thought was free and must
therefore achieve purity. Transposed into the literary realm,
this doctrine underwent transmutation and became responsible for the constant self-assertion and self-definition which
marked French Romanticism in poetry. Nature became the
confidant, the willing listener, the convenient outlet for outbursts of passion and splenetic emotion. The Romantics used
Nature as some of our contemporaries resort to psycho-
analysis in order to get rid of their inhibitions. Conversely,
Nature, which in Rousseau's eyes was a means to an end, became an end in itself, a value in itself. French Romanticism
in literature often assumed the attribute of a visual art.

It is not easy, nowadays, to avoid injustice in estimating the
contribution of the Romantics to French culture. Their pro-
ductive wealth and scope of interests has been unsurpassed.
Their ambitions exceeded those of the Encyclopedists in the
realm of knowledge. Their aspirations were truly Napoleonic.
They covered a tremendous area almost in the geographical
sense. Their imaginative wanderlust (for they travelled less
than Napoleon) introduced exotic conceptions, ideas, pictures:
they travelled by imagination, both in space and time. Their
social and political pursuits have been almost universal. Their
demagogic instincts (for they loved the people for its favours

as well as for itself) and their very egocentrism have certainly contrived to force culture and knowledge upon the public, even though it may have been in a half-digested form. They have aroused a wide rather than a deep curiosity. They have been cultural Tribunes of the People, and have shared its passions and emotions. Occasionally, this has produced such a master-piece as Hugo's *Les Misérables*, which remains a monument of human pity and charity. But they certainly have deserted the traditionally French occupation: the study of man and of life on their own merits. It will remain an open question whether their influence in the social field is a justification for a literary 'inflation' (as Léon Daudet called it) which makes their literary legacy more impressive by its bulk and universal preoccupa-tions than by its substance and density. That raises the problem of the true function of the writer or artist. The tradi-tional French answer to that question was the *séparation des pouvoirs*; the Romantics had chosen a different path.

In the field of literature and individual ethics, the test which can be applied to them is, after all, this: if a young French writer in the twentieth century looks for guidance, he will open Montaigne, Chamfort, or Stendhal rather than Hugo or Vigny; if he seeks a true example of poetical emotion, he will turn to Villon, Racine, Gérard de Nerval, or Rimbaud, rather than to Musset or Lamartine. This, of course, is a relative test. No absolute one can be applied.

The Romantic contribution was most valuable when it had sown its wild oats, when originally Romantic poets and writers returned to more classical forms, or amongst those men who, belonging in time and space to the Romantic era, partly adopted its style, but borrowed nothing from the orthodox movement. Hugo is more lasting in *Les Chansons des Rues et des Bois* or *Choses Vues* than in his early flights of self-expres-sion. Chateaubriand stands the test of time in *Les Mémoires d'Outre-Tombe*, worthy of Saint-Simon, better than in *Athala*. And Balzac, whose style occasionally suffers from Romantic prolixity, is the very personification of an intellectual and moral reaction against Romanticism.

In art, Romanticism turned out to be a considerable asset. Vision is the realm of the French. Departures from tradition in colourfulness only enriched the canvas, instead of provok-ing confusion. Indeed, they may be a valuable addition to the artist's statement. The Colourist revolution of Géricault and Delacroix certainly increased the artistic assets of Europe.

Romanticism produced a reaction not only when its influ-ence began to decline but also during its own time. The Romantics trespassed on every realm. The reaction was seen

in every field. The career of Ingres, a typically Classical painter, ran parallel with that of the Colourists, while other rebels
against the Romantic gospel included Stendhal, Balzac,
Gérard de Nerval, Mérimée, in the field of letters; Auguste
Comte, the exponent of Positivism, in philosophy; De Bonald
in sociology. Their reputation, in their own time, was not
equal to that of the Romantic reformers borne on the wings
of popularity. Neither Stendhal nor Balzac stimulated public
passion to the extent of arousing the scenes of mass controversy
which enlivened the première of Hugo's *Hernani*. Yet, after a
century has elapsed, French thought finds itself on firmer
ground in those works which retained the basic French qualities of direct communication, clear vision, and scrutiny of man's
fundamental motives, which analysed and described emotions without over-statement, than in the diffuse light of truly
romantic self-explanation and communion with an overgrown
Nature (a communion which Nerval ridiculed in his remark,
'Ils ont trop besoin de tutoyer l'ouragan'). One feels the solid
French bedrock and the true measure of human emotion in
Stendhal's *Chartreuse de Parme*. The classical simplicity of
Mérimée's *Carrosse du Saint-Sacrement* affords a safe refuge
from romantic eloquence. And Balzac's *Comédie Humaine*
is so comprehensive a world that it lives on, irrespective of
time or space, as a lasting human record. No man could ever
have seen more of man.

Many other names might of course be singled out in this
rich period known as the Romantic Era, which had also its
historians like Michelet and Thierry, and which produced
Berlioz in music. It is perhaps more interesting to assess
tendencies and changes in the cultural evolution of France
than to tabulate names and works, however outstanding.

The whole history of France between the Revolution and
the beginning of the twentieth century is a succession of oscilla-
tions from one political régime to another, from autocracy to
liberalism, from despotism to popular government. In their
own realm, literary and artistic schools as well as individuals
have been subject to similar fluctuations, sometimes under the
pressure of political phenomena, sometimes as reactions to
these, and sometimes independently of social or constitutional
evolution. Romanticism had been challenged and countered
at its height. The reaction was broader and more diverse at
the time of its decline, which approximately coincided with
the second part of the century.

The last spasm of Romanticism as an attitude of mind, and
perhaps also its greatest single poetical accomplishment, was
Baudelaire's *Fleurs du Mal*. By then, it had attained classical

E

form and classical harmony. Baudelaire is a case of exacerbated romanticism in ethics. Rousseau had asserted his faith in man, independently of faith in God. Baudelaire completed the cycle by the revolt of the individual against God. After him, Romanticism had exhausted its intellectual material as well as most of its specific means of expression.

The winding up of its affairs proved as complicated in literary and artistic terms as that of Charlemagne's Empire in terms of international politics. The divisions which followed and the multiplicity of schools which sprang up are, however, responsible for a cultural wealth equal to that of any previous period in French history. One romantic legacy (or perhaps simply a result of social evolution) survived: the interpenetration of literature and politics, with, however, the signal and shining exception of poetry, which returns to its own domain. The last decades of the nineteenth century rank as one of the richest poetical ages in the evolution of the French language, equal to any and second to none.

The first systematic reaction to Romanticism in poetry had been the 'School of Parnassus', which, in the second half of the century, attempted to restore its proper value and force to verbal expression and to a vocabulary weakened and loosened by the romantic habits of sonorous orchestration and visual exuberance. With the Parnassus, the poet ceased to be a Tribune of the People. This school, which produced Leconte de Lisle and Samain, does not, however, count amongst the greatest.

More was to come. Like the Napoleonic wars, the French defeat of 1871 had its poetical *Sturm und Drang* in a spiritual crisis which gave to France some of her purest poets. Never before had the French vocabulary been used with more skill, never had the versatile possibilities of its inflexions and terminations been as richly exploited as by those poets whom, in their own time, some critics described as decadent: Rimbaud above all, and with him or after him Verlaine, Mallarmé, Corbière, Laforgue, René Ghil. Poetry reacted against lyrical excesses. In the words of Verlaine 'it wrung the neck of eloquence'. It borrowed from music and painting, but it did so without leaving its own atmosphere, without losing sight of its own sphere. The poet applied to his art all the resources of language in sound and vision, but he did not seek inspiration elsewhere than in his own province, which is the expression or suggestion of emotions and desires that prose cannot translate. The Romantics had mainly used verse to amplify statements which prose could have rendered more simply and accurately. The long line of poets from Rimbaud to Guillaume Apolli-

naire, killed in the first World War, truly spoke the language
of poetry and could have spoken no other.

The age which, for want of a better word, may be described
as Post-Romantic, was even greater in painting. It was in fact
the most truly French age in the history of painting. From
Courbet and Corot to the great Impressionists, with Manet as
their herald, Degas, Cézanne, and chiefly Renoir as their highest interpreters, this period embodies some of the foremost
features of the French mind: passionate interest in the things
of life, clarity and independence of vision, acknowledgement
of reality, simplicity of statement. And this rich artistic era
also witnessed the rise of Auguste Rodin, a sculptor who can
compare with the giants of the Italian Renaissance, while the
turn of the century ushered in a host of French musicians who,
like Debussy, applied to their art the national qualities of
direct and limpid statement.

Unlike poetry and art, the novel, essays, fiction of all sorts,
continued to invade the field of politics and sociology. Social
aspirations and interests dominated all the works of Zola.
National mysticism found exponents in Barrès and Péguy,
inspired by the memory of 1871. Renan tried to assess the
values of his time and resumed the age-old search for an ethical
equilibrium between religious tradition and scientific evidence.
Anatole France adopted an attitude of total agnosticism defined
in the purest classical style. Alphonse Daudet, also a classic
in his means of expression, hesitated between conservatism
and progressive ideas. Journalism attracted writers and drew
them into the political arena. In the twentieth century, one
figure emerges as absolute heir to the individual moralist solely
preoccupied with the human person, its passions and its
motives: Marcel Proust, another name in the long tradition of
those whose fundamental object in art is the intelligence of man.

When the first Great War broke out, France's cultural
wealth and potentialities remained unimpaired. For nearly a
thousand years, in the balance of intellectual exchanges,
France retained a vast credit account.[1] Thought and language
remained clear. French civilization could still justly claim as
its motto: *Nihil quod humanum a me alienum puto.*

[1] Of this the above account is only a bare sketch. The names singled
out in this chapter have been chosen as indicative of tendencies or
specific qualities rather than for reasons of so-called 'precedence'.
Moreover, the whole contribution of France to scientific culture
(second to none and only rivalled by that of the British) has been left
out of consideration for want of both space and qualifications for the
task. So also has the part played by the French in economic
thought. It must be understood that the object of this brief outline is
not to ascribe to France a certain 'rank' in civilization but to point out
some characteristics of French culture.

OCCUPIED
and
UNOCCUPIED
FRANCE
June 1940

Dunkirk
Calais
Boulogne
Lille
Cherbourg
Dieppe
Amiens
Havre
Honfleur
Rouen
Reims
R. Meuse
Metz
Caen
Nancy
Granville
PARIS
Brest
St. Malo
OCCUPIED
FRANCE
Strasbourg
Quimper
Rennes
Orleans
R. Seine
Lorient
St. Nazaire
Tours
R. Loire
Dijon
Besançon
Nantes
F R A N C E
La Rochelle
VICHY
Rochefort
Limoges
LYONS
St. Etienne
Grenoble
Pauillac
R. Dordogne
BORDEAUX
UNOCCUPIED FRANCE
Arcachon
R. Garonne
Mentone
Biarritz
Bayonne
Montpellier
R. Rhone
Nice
Cannes
Toulouse
Sète
St. Tropez
Agde
MARSEILLES
Narbonne
Toulon
Perpignan

II. THE FRENCH CRISIS IN THE TWENTIETH CENTURY

In 1939, France, once more in her history, was called upon to fulfil her historic mission: that of a living bulwark of Western civilization against tribal migrations from beyond the Rhine. In June 1940 the military and civil framework broke down under the German impact.

The resistance of a nation at war to a foreign onslaught does not depend upon the individual spirit of its citizens only: it is the result of a long process, the organization and marshalling of its power in men, material, knowledge, and external friends.

The individual Frenchman was as conscious of the meaning of German expansion in 1939 as in 1914. But the national framework did not prove adequate to the traditional task. The explanation is not to be found in May or June 1940 but in a period covering more than twenty years—and in many fields.

CHAPTER V

DEMOGRAPHIC POWER AND INTERNATIONAL POLICY

D
URING the years which preceded or heralded the present
conflict, a German diplomat in London had a ready
answer for those who asked him whether he feared an
outbreak of hostilities: 'A second World War? Impossible.
There can't possibly be two World Wars within a lifetime.'
Consciously or not, he was expressing the official German conviction that the Western Powers were unable to stand the
strain of a second struggle twenty years after the holocaust of
1914–18.

This conviction was not founded on irresponsible calculations. Like most apparently naïve slogans propagated by German agents, it was based on a minute study of social biology
in Europe. War being the chief German industry, all the problems connected with it are studied with a thoroughness un-
dreamed of in any other country. Chief among these problems,
in the German estimation, was the relative importance attached
by each European nation to the preservation of human lives,
of human blood. For each single country this importance
grows in inverse ratio to its man-power. It must be particularly great for those who have to maintain a prominent place
in the world with temporarily limited means.

European nations, for the Germans, are not abstract geographical notions: their organic life is scrutinized more closely
than their outward manifestations. The organic life of a people
is the number, age, state of health, and various potentialities
of its citizens capable of bearing arms. Just as a weak patient
is more vulnerable than a man in a sound condition, the Germans calculate that a nation at a low ebb in terms of youthful
man-power will show at the same time less resistance and less
preparedness for a long war than an over-populous community.

The great fear of the Germans has always been Russia.
Although the main German objective in our times has been the
destruction of the West and of Western Civilization, which is
most antagonistic to them, Russia represented both a greater
danger and a more desirable prey. Colonized and dominated,
the vast numbers of her population would be an asset to Germany. A strong and independent Russia is dreaded by Germany, for her demographic problem can have no bearing upon
her international attitude. She was therefore, in 1939, the
main German preoccupation.

Great Britain, from a German point of view was, in terms of

demography, a case apart. She might or might not be influenced by considerations of self-preservation. But England was not directly accessible by land. She could on the whole determine for herself, even in the midst of war, the extent of her sacrifice in man-power, because she was not compelled to rush her whole manhood to the frontiers. To a great extent she could regulate and control her own participation.

France was the main object of German social-biological study. France relatively to her population had been the main sufferer from the last war. She had not recovered from it. With a vast Empire, a static birth-rate, and heavy defensive obligations on three frontiers, she would hesitate to make extensive sacrifices which might save her once more but would leave her biologically exhausted, possibly incapable of keeping her rank in Europe and of maintaining her hold on a vast Empire. At the same time, she was the hinge of any Allied system of operations against Germany. That the Germans thought along those lines is clearly shown by their propaganda to France at the beginning of the present war. This propaganda was not based on a hope of individual defeatism. It did not say 'Why lose your lives for a worthless cause?' It said: 'Why compromise the future of the nation by a huge sacrifice of blood for the sake of others?' Hence the repeated allegation that in every war France would pay the highest tribute, fall into national decay through anaemia, and lose her place in the world to countries who had taken a lesser share in the struggle.

Finally, it must be emphasized that the Germans are perfectly conscious of the demographic problem in their own country. Hitler's assertion to Burckardt that he would readily sacrifice ten million men to achieve victory betrayed an insane unconsciousness of that problem, for not even Germany can bear such a sacrifice without fatal consequences. That Hitler was ready to stake all on a German military victory is probable. That his readiness to do so has been a constant subject of alarm to the traditionalists who have a longer-term conception of German history is absolutely certain. It was in order to calm their fears that month after month Hitler played down the German losses in Russia, or, alternatively, to make such sacrifices acceptable, repeatedly sought to justify them by over-emphasizing the alleged threats of total extinction which Germany had to face. The German method of mechanical warfare, when successful, is not costly in human lives. And until the Russian campaign the superiority complex of the German soldier was due to his feeling of relative security against other combatants through the provision of material which, in attack as well as in defence, was a shield as much as a weapon. To-day, when the Allies have achieved superiority in available material, the Germans think in terms of men far more than in terms of machines. The superiority of a small mechanized army over a large number of under-armed men is a fact. Once equality is restored in weapons the demographic problem arises with the same acuteness as in previous wars and probably even more so. Those who doubt it will be enlightened by the publication of German casualties in this war when the list is complete. The Germans must know them. They may now remember that after the Thirty Years War it took Germany nearly a hundred years to play a decisive part in European affairs.

Although France has seldom spent more than twenty years of her national history without being engaged in some conflict, she only became conscious of the demographic problem at the turn of the last century, and acutely aware of it during the first World War. It is not sufficiently realized that the policy followed by the 'strong' governments which followed the war and later in 1934 by statesmen like Louis Barthou was essentially founded on the notion of demographic weakness.

The relation between man-power and international policy may be better understood with the help of a few figures. According to the official records of the American War Department, the French casualties during the first World War stood at: officially killed, 1,357,000; wounded, 4,266,000; missing, 537,000 (of whom over 200,000 were in fact dead). The total figure amounts to 73 per cent. of the number of men mobilized in four years and three months of war, i.e. 8,410,000. (In Great Britain the proportion was 35·8 per cent.) Out of this total, nearly one million men were maimed, and several hundred thousands partly disabled. It is therefore not surprising that in 1939, in spite of the recovery of Alsace-Lorraine, the French-born population of France should not have exceeded the 1913 figure. Yet the census is misleading, for it supplies a total figure of population which is partly irrelevant in terms of man-power. In 1939, the male population capable of active service was very noticeably below the 1913 figure; the classes of conscripts called to the colours were only beginning to equal those of 1913, and the reserves, in terms of able-bodied men, could only have reached the 1913 figure towards 1950. Finally, part of the able-bodied population had been directly under the physical and moral strain of the previous war. It is quite clear that in 1939 the cumulative effect of all these factors was still telling heavily on the French nation.

From the 1918 Armistice onwards, the policy of France was

governed by the notion of demographic power and guided by the consciousness of the figures just set out. Germany had been defeated. But those men who were responsible for French policy did not consider the German threat on its present merits but on its future potentialities.

In this, the French followed their traditional line of thought. Germany's ambitions might be assuaged in the future. But the fate of France could not be entrusted to such a hypothetical process. Mathematically, a nation of less than forty million inhabitants, cannot, other things being equal, fight on even terms a country of nearly seventy millions whose industrial output is vastly superior to her own. French policy at the end of the last war was based on this fundamental truth.

There were three methods by which Germany's initial advantage could be offset: the setting-up of a collective system of security; the maintenance by France of a considerable margin of technical superiority in armaments; the conclusion of alliances with foreign countries, on the principle of balance of power. The history of France between 1918 and 1938 spells a succession of failures in every one of these attempts.

The true charter of collective security was the Covenant of the League of Nations. This instrument lacked operative clauses. Moreover, it was rejected by the United States Senate. In order to strengthen the Covenant and to turn it into an instrument of immediate and practical value in case of emergency, France instigated the drafting of the Geneva Protocol, which afforded sufficient means of coercion to be a true deterrent to aggression. It was adopted by the Assembly of the League on the 2nd October 1924, subject to ratification by the various governments. It was rejected by Great Britain on the 12th March 1925. As a partial compensation, Great Britain later undertook by the Treaty of Locarno to guarantee France's northern frontiers. The main drawback of this instrument, as against a wider guarantee, was that its value was merely local and could only be tested at the last minute. It was not preventive.

In the opinion of the French, the Treaty of Locarno was a valuable asset. But Great Britain at the time was not a military power. In order to prevent the Franco-German issue from being reduced to a problem of comparative man-power, France still had to maintain absolute superiority in armaments over the German Reich. Moreover, she could not without it enforce the execution of the financial clauses of the Versailles Treaty by Germany. To Anglo-Saxon opinion these clauses appeared harsh, and when France occupied the Ruhr in order to secure their execution, her initiative was severely judged. It may

70 FRANCE

be useful to recall in this respect that in less than two years after June 1940 France paid over to Germany in absolute value more than Germany had paid to France in ten years after the first World War. The sum total of German extortions since cannot yet be calculated, but it must be fabulous.

As long as Germany remained relatively disarmed, not only could France hope to secure payment[1] but, what was far more important, she could continue to live without fear.

For a period of over twelve years, France's international position remained strong. In 1932, the process of revision of the Versailles Treaty and of Germany's international status began in earnest. For a long time the Anglo-Saxon nations had been suggesting an alteration of its financial clauses and a reform of its military stipulations. They urged France to agree both to a further alleviation of Germany's financial burden, which had already been substantially reduced, and to equality of armaments as between France and Germany.

Irrespective of their political tendencies, the successive French Governments linked the problem of armaments with that of effective international guarantees. Concessions could only be granted to Germany in the military sphere in so far as France received an equivalent in terms of security. For several years the 'reconciliation between the German demand for equality and the French demand for security'[2] became the chief aim of British statesmen and diplomats.

It may be that the retention of powerful armaments seemed to give France European predominance. However, the means at her disposal were backed by a limited, conservative, and static population: their purpose was to balance the weight of a nation superficially weak but potentially formidable and traditionally expansionist. In appearance, equality of rights between France and Germany was in conformity with a true policy of balance of power (apart from its ideological merits). Yet this equilibrium was only apparent. It was an 'equilibrium' between nations which did not take into account either their respective populations or their respective weights in terms of industrial strength. Once Germany had achieved parity with France no force in Europe could prevent her from exploiting her industry and man-power to the full.

France therefore refused mathematical equality in armaments without effective international guarantees and control.

[1] In fact, independently of her own payments to Great Britain and the U.S.A., France spent twice as much on the restoration of her devastated territory as she received from Germany.
[2] This is an actual quotation from several speeches by Sir John (now Lord) Simon in 1932 and 1933.

After an attempt to reach a compromise on the subject, this refusal became final on the 17th April 1934, when Louis Barthou sent a note to the members of the League Council. On the other hand, she had in 1932 agreed to the relief of Germany's financial burden. It is sometimes contended that Hitler's success in Germany is the direct result of French resistance to German demands, and of the hardships suffered by Germany under the financial clauses of the Versailles Treaty. With regard to Germany's payments, they amounted in fact to an average of less than 1·5 per cent. of her national revenue[1] and remained vastly inferior to the credits invested in the Reich by the former Allied powers. With regard to armaments, the posthumous publication of Stresemann's *Notebooks* has shown that the policy of this 'peaceful' statesman differed from Hitler's only in means, methods of approach, and time, and that his aims were not noticeably dissimilar. Grievances, as such, do not turn a peaceful community into an irrepressibly expansionist nation. The sense of defeat had a far greater influence upon German psychology than the so-called injustices of the Versailles Treaty. In other words, revenge rather than redress of wrongs proved a spur to the German spirit.

Barthou's note was not the only manifestation of French policy in face of the German problem, which by then had become acute, since Hitler was in power. France hastened to strengthen her links with those continental States which lay exposed to the German menace. Moreover, for the first time since Brest-Litovsk, she undertook to revise her relations with Russia. Negotiations were initiated for the conclusion of a pact with the U.S.S.R. This scheme did not meet with the approval of France's natural ally, Great Britain. However, until 1935, France succeeded in maintaining her relative superiority over Germany by virtue of her armaments and of the system of alliances which she had built as a substitute for a collective pact of effective, and not merely theoretical, security.

The decline of France's international power began in 1935, and, incidentally, Laval was its main engineer. Laval undermined the French framework of continental alliances, emasculated the Franco-Russian Pact before he signed it and eventually prevented its ratification by the French Parliament. Meanwhile he alienated the goodwill of Great Britain by his opposition to the enforcement of sanctions against the Italian aggressor. It must be said, nevertheless, that Laval's policy on the question of sanctions was tolerated in France only because public opinion had been constantly disappointed in its hopes of

[1] Statistics supplied by the German *Wirtschaft und Statistik*.

securing the firm support of Great Britain against the permanent German danger; and, above all, because French public opinion had been staggered by the conclusion of the naval treaty between England and Nazi Germany.

The sequence of events between 1931 and 1936 illustrates more strikingly than at any other period in history how differences between England and France can lead to fatal results in the face of a recurrent German threat. Ever since the Armistice France had founded her policy on the notion of German expansionism irrespective of Germany's temporary weakness. Throughout the same period of years England had acted upon a conception of balance of power which ignored the demographic weight of Germany and only considered her accidental inferiority. When the problem of collective security arose in a practical form on an issue which was not the German one, France hesitated to follow the British lead unless England gave her effective guarantees against the Reich. And finally, when Hitler reoccupied the Rhineland, Great Britain was opposed to any retaliatory action and, by then, France, internally and externally weakened, had lost her grip on events and her sense of direction: she did not chose to act alone against British advice and missed the last opportunity of checking the growing power of Germany before it was too late.

The demilitarized zone of the Rhine was a vital asset to the Western Powers. Nearly three centuries before, Turenne had established by more brutal methods a similar sort of 'no man's land' between France and Germany by devastating the Palatinate. The Versailles Treaty had operated in a more civilized way, but the need was the same in 1936 as in the seventeenth century. Yet public opinion in many countries argued that 'after all it was German land'. Later, the same public opinion agreed that 'the Austrians were Germans', that 'the Sudetens were Germans', until it had to acknowledge the fact that German expansionism was going forward irrespective of languages, boundaries, rights, and interests—until it had to face the fact that German grievances are not founded on the notion of right or wrong but are part of Germany's arsenal of multifarious weapons.

After 1936, the balance of power between France and Germany had been decisively upset in favour of the Reich. Nothing could prevent Germany from marshalling her industrial power and from building up her strength in direct proportion to her vast population and huge industrial equipment. This equipment was indeed sufficient, for whereas in the years which had followed her defeat Germany had not been able to pay for the havoc which she had wrought in France, she had

IV. IN THE FIELDS

absorbed and utilized the large credits granted to her by
England and America. Even her naval yards were not idle.
The naval treaty which she had concluded with England in
June 1935 was but an instrument in her hands to justify an
unbounded activity in that field.

Spain, Austria, the Sudetenland, Czechoslovakia: everywhere Germany advanced, unchecked. In 1938, the only
superiority of France over Germany was in the number of
trained reserves. Germany had succeeded in achieving that
equality which she had claimed for so long and which meant
in fact a tremendous superiority over any single power (apart
from Russia) since France would henceforth be faced with the
inexorable law of numbers and potential output. She had
attempted to break that law by methods of compulsion and by
international contracts. Because of the opposition which her
policy encountered on the part of her former Allies and
eventually through her own failings, France's endeavours had
been frustrated.

In 1939 these memories were vivid in the minds of the
French people. They remembered that twenty years ago their
country had emerged victorious from a desperate conflict with
a stronger military power, that its security could only endure
so long as the inequality of forces was compensated by technical and political superiority over Germany, that France's former allies had watched the rebirth of German might for twenty
years without preventing it, and that, finally, the French
nation, still suffering from its old wounds, would have to stand
in the path of a full-grown Germany twice as strong as France
in population, three times as strong in industrial resources.
This knowledge did not affect the attitude of the individual
Frenchman at the outbreak of hostilities. He was ready to
make the recurrent sacrifice, but he was equally conscious of
the fact that France was fulfilling her traditional mission in the
worst possible circumstances. This feeling played little part in
the early months of the conflict, nor did it impair confidence
in the outcome. But it existed in a latent form, together with
a sense of loneliness in bearing a burden for which his own
country's past blunders were not exclusively responsible. He
saw the inroads made in his own ranks by the recent conflict,
and he did not see Europe standing by his side.

CHAPTER VI

TRADITIONAL ASSETS TURNED INTO LIABILITIES

IN terms of numbers, the problem set to France was serious enough. Unless she received considerable military support from her allies she would have to fulfil her mission in conditions of unprecedented numerical inferiority. On demographic grounds alone there was a wide discrepancy between France's traditional role and her present internal strength. The economic status of France as against other great Powers raised an equally grave issue: there again the contrast was marked between the task and the means.

Historically, the geographical diversity of France and her balanced economy had proved to be valuable assets. Wars could ravage her territory: a few years later the country would regain its prosperity and resume its poise, like the sea after a storm, without any trace of turmoil. As Montesquieu wrote: 'One of the things which must be noted in France is the supreme facility with which she always recovers from her losses, diseases, casualties, and the resilience with which she always withstands or even overcomes the vices of her various governments. It may well be that she owes this faculty to her very diversity which does not allow any evil to take root and destroy the fruit of her natural advantages.'

It is true that, given the peaceful enjoyment of these advantages, France has been able in the past to surmount any crisis due to the deficiencies or shortcomings of her leaders. But in the twentieth century she had not only lost her demographic wealth at a time when the German population reached the figure of eighty millions: her 'natural advantages' themselves had ceased to be an asset and had turned into a serious liability.

France in the twentieth century remained primarily an agricultural country. Industry in France had grown according to a slow process of evolution and not by leaps and bounds as it had in England during the nineteenth century, and even more so in Germany during the last seventy-five years. Industrial development was not a paramount necessity in France. Industry had therefore progressed somewhat at leisure, seeking favourable conditions and pursuing quality rather than quantity. In the years which preceded the present war, small concerns acted as a brake on industrial expansion and standardization upon a modern scale. In 1931 60 per cent. of the French industrial population worked in firms employing less than twenty persons. France's most powerful industries themselves were born from her 'natural advantages'. Thus the existence on her territory of the largest iron mines in western Europe was responsible for her great progress in heavy industries and foundries, just as, centuries before, a region favourable to the acclimatization of silkworms had given Lyons its rich silk-weaving industry.

The maintenance of a vast land army had kept up industries which had to meet the requirements of national defence. Even in this respect, industrial development was guided by academic conceptions of warfare. Traditionally, the defence departments counted more, for instance, on heavy than on mechanical industries. Should the traditional conceptions be upset (as they were), there was no reserve of industrial power in France immediately and conveniently adaptable to new contingencies. To give an example, had the French found themselves in the same predicament as the British in June 1940, they could not have drawn from their industrial equipment and skilled labour, through a mere process of technical adaptation, what the British were able to draw from their mechanical industries in terms of planes and other weapons in anything like so short a time. In 1918, a tremendous effort had been made in this respect with great success, but the elements of the problem, especially in aircraft construction, were then totally different.

As early as 1913 the ratio of industrial potential as between Germany, England, and France, was computed at: Germany 3, England 2, France 1. The margin of difference between France and Germany can only have increased in the last ten years, as, from 1933 to 1939, the Germans exploited their resources to the full by compulsory methods and spent on war equipment in six years three times as much as France had in twenty.

The relative industrial weakness of France amongst the great Powers is easily explained: Industry in France has progressed according to the needs of the internal market and not as in England, where to export is vital. In peace time, apart from the equipment and supply of her army, France was under no obligation to produce more than the requirements of her internal market. She never attempted to export on such a scale as Germany or England. An industrial development which is not the result of a commanding necessity seldom attains its highest degree of expansion and efficiency.

On the other hand, the agricultural tradition in France remained strong: historically, because the peasantry had always been the backbone of the nation, and practically, because in cases of emergency the land guaranteed national self-sufficiency and provided a sound reservoir of man-power.

Although in 1931[1] the number of land workers was slightly less than that of persons employed in trade and industry (the ratio was about four to five), the people actually leading a rural or semi-rural life were still a majority by a very narrow margin. Between land and urban population, the balance was on the whole maintained.

The possibility that this equilibrium might be impaired was a great source of preoccupation to French statesmen. One of their main fears, especially after the first World War, was the flight from the land. In the early 'twenties, country folk had shown some tendency to emigrate towards industry and, generally, cities. In fact the process never assumed alarming proportions. Nevertheless it was thought that in the national interest any such movement should be checked. French leaders and politicians dreaded the evil of unemployment and, above all, they attached the greatest importance to the preservation of a numerical balance between industry and agriculture.

Even those among them who realized the need for industrial development suggested solutions which would not upset the equilibrium: for instance, the elimination of small industrial concerns and their merger into larger ones, or a substantial progress in the electrification of the land, which would stimulate industry without affecting the balance of population. The protection of this precarious balance was an article of faith for almost every Frenchman.

Considered in general terms and according to apparent logic, such a conception was sound. It was in conformity with tradition, social ethics, and orthodox economy. In any case, no sudden departure from this national doctrine could have been made without a social crisis even worse than that which France underwent during the last ten years.

Yet this so-called balance, with all its implications in the economic and social fields, proved to be a capital factor of the French crisis in the twentieth century. Sound and rational from an absolute point of view, it turned out to be a source of fundamental weakness in terms of national power, and under international conditions of a revolutionary nature.

By current standards, France seems an ideal ground for experiments in self-sufficiency, whilst Germany seems to be the worst possible one. Self-sufficiency in France would not substantially impair the minimum standards of feeding and health. A policy of autarky in Germany was never thought conceivable. According to accepted economic principles, it

[1] The date of the latest statistics available in the country.

F

would inaugurate a reign of *ersatz* and underfeeding with its
consequent toll on health and physical resistance. All this is
true, but it simply means that autarky as an end in itself and
for a long period of years is not biologically practicable in
Germany.

As a temporary means of building a tremendous war machine
it is an entirely different proposition. Whilst autarky, in a
basically industrial country like Germany, whose land resources
are inadequate to the population, may destroy the race in a few
generations, it is even clearer that the bullet manufactured in
this economically monstrous system will kill in a fraction of a
second the most healthy type of French peasant. The autarkic
system is, of course, merely a weapon. Once this weapon has
achieved its purpose, the agricultural wealth of Europe is there
to raise anew the standards of German living long before the
effects of economic autarky have begun to tell on Germany
Out of the 1,400,000 French prisoners, there are some 800,000
once-sturdy peasants whose sojourn in German prison camps
will leave a scar on the body of France, whilst for years
ersatz-fed Teutons have been able to recuperate through
their pillaging of the richest land in Europe. Such are the
real terms of the question. On the basis of orthodox economy
autarky is only practicable in a well-balanced country. When
war is the main purpose and economy a temporary means
to an end, an autarkic system proves to be incomparably
superior to a balanced national unit.[1] In fact, in times of
war, the natural process in any country is to encourage and
even force industrial development and to reduce the standards
of living. What Germany has done in the last ten years is
merely to anticipate this process in time of peace.

In 1939 no statesmanship and no departure from policy
could have altered the fact that by reason of the nature of the
balance between the urban and the rural population of France,
the war-potential of Germany once released and exploited to
the full would prove to be several times greater than that of
France. The initial industrial ratio of one to three probably
became a ratio of one to four or one to five. In the last war,
only the division of German resources, the relatively lesser
degree of her industrial mobilization, and the utmost exertions
on the part of France and her allies eventually succeeded in
overcoming the industrial might of Germany.

Independently of political mistakes and failures in securing
at least the maximum output consistent with French industrial
means during the last ten years, there was therefore a funda-

[1] In the last war Germany became autarkic under compulsion.
Hitler had merely turned a necessity into a deliberate policy.

V. CON-
STRUCTION

**1. MARÈGES
DAM**

**2. A BRIDGE
IN FINISTÈRE**

mental weakness in the French economy considered in terms
of power and war potential. This, however, was not the only
drawback of an economy still founded in the twentieth century
on the traditional exploitation of natural advantages. The
French land is, on the whole, capable of feeding its forty million inhabitants: which means that its agricultural output in
every direction is more or less adequate to the requirements of
forty million persons. This land was directly or indirectly
exploited by some eighteen million French men and women
leading a rural or semi-rural life and thus had to provide them
with means of subsistence on twentieth-century standards. It
is clear that the prices of produce of all descriptions as well as
cattle, fowls, and livestock, had to be worked out so as to be
remunerative for this considerable section of the French
population.

In Canada, the Argentine, the U.S.A., and Australia, infi-
nitely vaster lands, equally rich, were exploited by a relatively
smaller number of people. The result was that in those countries the same number of bushels of wheat or head of cattle, for
instance, had only to provide a means of living for a far smaller
number of producers. To take an example: the agricultural
population of Canada numbers slightly more than five millions.
The production of wheat in a good year (1939) is 489,625,000
bushels. French production in equally favourable circumstances amounts to about 340,000,000 bushels. Admittedly,
the ratio of wheat-growers to the total agricultural population is
higher in Canada than it is in France. Nevertheless, it remains
true on the whole that with a smaller output France had to
provide remunerative prices for a far larger population than
Canada. And this applied to most cereals, to cattle, in fact to
practically everything produced by the French land, with the
exception of wine and tobacco.

The result is obvious: the produce of France was bound to
be considerably more expensive than that of any of the big
agricultural countries overseas if it had to ensure the subsistence of the French rural population. Consequently remunerative prices in France could only be secured through
various forms of protection ranging from tariffs and quotas to
direct government subsidies. This turned out to be one of the
effects of France's 'natural advantages'. From 1929 onwards,
effective protection was enforced by various means, culmi-
nating, in 1936, in the grant of heavy subsidies. This became
a feature of French commercial policy. In other words, apart
from the international consequences of protection, France had
to burden her Exchequer and to restrict her expenditure in
other fields in order to maintain on the land a population

which in terms of current world-economy could not live on it profitably and normally. To stretch the point even further, whilst Germany was practising industrial autarky in order to win the war which she was actively preparing, France weakened her economy by practising a form of purely traditional and conservative autarky.

Nor was this all. Protectionism had to become effective even at the expense of the French Empire. This could not be avoided without reducing producers to semi-starvation. Despite their cheapness in terms of world prices, French wines, vegetable oils, tobacco, and the like, were expensive as compared with their Algerian and Tunisian equivalents. Again, prices in France had to be fixed in accordance with the basic needs of the home producer, which were naturally higher than those of the Empire producer—as the latter not only employed cheaper labour, but resorted to modern methods of exploitation.

This picture of the industrial inadequacy of France, as against some other world powers, and of her over-burdened agriculture, is not intended to suggest that France's natural advantages had ceased to be an asset and a source of strength in the present century. It simply means that in terms of population the traditional balance would have had to be altered. It means that whilst France must retain her natural wealth, this wealth should have been exploited on methods of greater efficiency by a more limited number of people. The remedy should have been a rational and controlled exodus from the land towards industry, which was precisely the very process which every French Government attempted to check.

Not only would such an evolution have relieved agriculture of an excessive burden, but it would have reinforced industry and would have had as its consequences the increase of France's industrial power and the provision of modern farm machinery permitting adequate exploitation of the land. A true policy of economic balance adapted to twentieth-century demands would have followed that line instead of using artificial means to maintain the maximum number of people on the land. Such a bold policy, challenging tradition and even popular feeling, would admittedly have provoked the strongest hostile reactions. It may be that nothing short of a revolution could have enforced it. In 1939 an economist, M. Dufretay, was writing thus: 'In the pursuit of any economic policy, the only guide, for the central authorities, has been hitherto the number of electors interested in agricultural production.' This remark reveals both the political motives of some conservative economists in France and the fears which any idea of reform aroused in the minds of French leaders.[1]

The need for greater industrial development was none the less evident to most statesmen. Even within the limits set by the determination to maintain and protect an economically excessive agricultural population, there was still considerable scope. Basically and without recruiting men outside of its own ranks, French industry could have been considerably improved in output and potential by a process of concentration. This process, which has marked the evolution of most industrial countries during the last hundred years, has been encouraged in America with peaceful aims, and in Germany for warlike purposes.

Although industrial concentration runs counter to French instincts and ways of life, private enterprise took bold steps in that direction between 1919 and 1939. These individual efforts were not popular. In 1930, a leading French writer, Georges Duhamel, published a scathing satire on America's mechanized industry and life as a warning against such a process of evolution. And it is significant of the French attitude to the problem that not only did the book become a bestseller, but that it drew upon its author the hitherto grudged favours of the French Academy.

Nevertheless, concentration went on, stimulated by motor magnates such as Citröen and Renault. In those concerns, which followed the American pattern, success was complete. Such progress, however, was somewhat belated. In 1939, the process of concentration in France was far from adequate to the country's requirements, in terms of power if not of peaceful economy.

A form of industrial development which appealed more generally to the French was the scheme of electrification of the land. Here was a method of tackling the industrial problem which had the advantage of being practicable without causing substantial displacements of population; hence the general favour with which it soon met, in spite of some resistance amongst the peasantry in its first stage. The results achieved in that direction in twenty years were remarkable. The building of such masterpieces of engineering as the dams of Eguzon, Marèges, and others, marked a considerable advance. Whole

[1] This argument relates only to the imperative necessities of France's actual situation and her immediate future and does not at all purport to enter into the controversy relating to the advantages and disadvantages of a concentrated factory organization as against a basically rural way of life. Clearly any wholesale concentration would require as a minimum compensation a bold policy of periodic dispersion for education and leisure.

railway tracks were electrified on networks totalling several thousand miles. Farms and country houses passed from the age of the oil, to that of the electric, lamp.

Had these various methods of improving production been generally adopted, the need for a revolution against traditional economy would still have been imperative at a time when French statesmen should have considered economic issues not as an end in themselves but in their relation to international power. Instead of this, the curve of industrial output in France showed a slight drop between 1932 and 1938, whilst British production was increasing and German production trebling. For this drop, the social crisis which France underwent during the last years of peace was partly responsible—although it remains doubtful whether the curve could, in any case, have been redressed to the extent of substantially altering the ratio of Franco-German industrial power.

CHAPTER VII

AN ENDEMIC REVOLUTION

IT is a common phenomenon amongst civilized nations that when their very existence is threatened by an external foe they forget their internal dissensions and compose their differences. This reaction to national emergency is naturally held to be a healthy sign of national feeling. However, the implications of this phenomenon may be overlooked. Fortunately or unfortunately, divergences between men and parties are part of the life of a nation and of its evolution. Unanimity in the face of the enemy, which is essential to the survival of a country, amounts at the same time to an interruption of its normal process of evolution. For it does not solve all problems but merely postpones their solution.

It may and does happen that internal disputes and internal unrest have causes so profound and roots so deep, that they take precedence over the national interest even in cases of emergency. This does not necessarily import a general attitude of irresponsibility on the part of the nation concerned. It may suggest that the imperative demands of evolution have not been met and that adjustments have been too long delayed.

In 1938, the alarm of Munich had not altogether succeeded in eliminating the elements of the French internal crisis which had been manifest since 1934 and even before. It took the full-scale mobilization of September 1939 to complete the national reconciliation. The response of the people was total. Nevertheless, the wounds had been dressed rather than healed and had affected the national life and especially the country's production. The purpose of this book is not to pass judgement on the respective merits of the grievances and claims advanced by parties and men, but to record a number of features of the crisis. Let it be said that, irrespective of individual rights and wrongs, the Popular Front certainly corresponded to at least one aspect of French evolution.

The factors in the French crisis are extremely complex because France suffered at the same time from the social difficulties which attended most European states during the last few decades and also from others peculiar to herself which the previous conflict had left unsolved. The last ten years or so have shown that there exists an inherent and fundamental contradiction within a nation between the notion of power and the notion of individual freedom. The curbing of individual tendencies and aspirations has proved as deadly a war-weapon in the hands of Germany as her methods of autarkic coercion. Conversely, in democratic countries, the war has imposed limitations of all sorts on individual self-expression. It is only through freedom that conflicting tendencies and varying grievances can be given utterance, and those are part of a process of evolution. It may be said in this respect, that in France democracy suffered to the utmost in the last twenty years through allowing an unusual degree of freedom in the pressing of claims and through doing far less than was needed to remedy the fundamental shortcomings of her social organization. In other words, she allowed social evolution to manifest itself in its most acute forms and in complete freedom of expression without seriously endeavouring to meet its profound requirements. On both counts, the chief sufferer was the power of the State—as, after all, individual life in France could remain tolerably pleasant in almost any circumstances, and even in the midst of social unrest.

What were the basic factors of social evolution in France?

In all parts of Europe, the growth and concentration of industry throughout the nineteenth century produced the class which is commonly described as 'the proletariat'. As against 'the common people' of old, the industrial proletariat may be truly considered as a class, because most of its members share a number of recognizable features and interests. They live exclusively on wages and not on the exploitation of personal assets such as land, trade, workshop or business. Their means of livelihood are, originally at least, determined by their employer, not necessarily in direct ratio to his own prosperity (hence the need for trade union protection). Finally and chiefly, their work is collective and not individual. The traditional claims of the proletariat are the exact reflection of these distinctive features and interests: demands for security which the nature of their income renders precarious, insistence on the establishment of a constant relation between their wages and the profits derived from their work, the right to take collective action in the assertion of their claims.

The specific problems raised by the existence and growth of the proletariat have been understood and dealt with in different ways by different states. In France, industrial progress was slower and smoother than in England, Germany, or the United States. Despite the spread of trade unionism the social issue was never faced and treated in a comprehensive fashion. Trade unionism never enjoyed the status nor the membership which it has in Great Britain. Even after the Great War, a considerable number of industrial concerns fixed the rates of wages without any reference to economic conditions or to prevailing practice. This was one of the causes of the social crisis.

It may seem paradoxical that the French nation, which had been the first to transform the ancient social order, should in many respects have been found lagging behind others in the field of social reform. Yet this paradox can be explained simply enough. The French, who had experienced a century of setbacks before the permanently achieved constitutional liberalism, were still living after the Great War on the tradition of their great social transformation. They were inclined to believe that its teachings supplied an answer to most problems—except, of course, those men who hoped for a return to monarchical rule. Having stated that men were born free and equal in rights, having abolished privileges of birth, destroyed ancient shackles to man's initiative, regulated community life by laws applying to all citizens, introduced universal suffrage, free education for all, and such like, the natural tendency of the true heirs to the Revolution was to trust in these fundamental principles for the settlement of most problems. These heirs belonged to most parties: for it is a significant oddity of French parliamentary life that every group, from the extreme right to the socialists, appealed to the 'ideas' of the French Revolution, either in support of their most trivial political moves or against any of their opponents' suggestions.

In those men who professed it, faith in an ideology born of eighteenth-century concepts resulted in a conservative attitude to modern problems. The principles of the great Revolution, however valid they remain in terms of human ethics, can no more supply an answer to economic questions arising in 1939 than sincere belief in Revelation can suffice to solve an equation of the second degree.

Moreover, the legacy from 1789 was particularly inadequate to modern conditions where the status of the proletariat was concerned. In 1789 one of the essential popular claims was the right of every Frenchman to acquire and retain private property: whereas the demands for security of the wage-earning class in the twentieth century assume forms very different from that of a claim for land or even property.

Whilst the French revolutionary tradition could hardly contribute to the solution of problems created by the existence of an industrial class, because it was definitely behind the times, it was hardly more helpful in the case of the peasantry. The peasantry's difficulties proceeded not from any challenge to their historical rights but from the discrepancy between French and world prices. This was an entirely new economic issue. The interests of the peasantry were if anything rather contrary to the liberal economic principles of the Revolution, for they might have been better served by a return to economic regionism. On the whole, the Revolution had left a valuable inheritance in the shape of a mental approach to political questions. In order to solve the difficulties inherent in the economic situation of France in a post-war world, French statesmanship would have needed, however, a new and completely unprejudiced outlook.

In terms of parliamentary politics, the French system of parties was altogether anachronistic. In the normal course of events, parties are born of common practical needs. Their programmes are the expression of the needs of their members, as well as of personal conceptions of the national interest and of the best way of serving it. Not so in France. In most cases, French parties presented to the eye a strange kaleidoscope in which every single colour had some far-flung origin in historical events, wholly irrelevant to the existing situation. These parties were like the luminous rays of those stars whose light only reaches us some hundred years after the star itself is extinguished. The majority of members in any French parliament represented rural or semi-rural constituencies. They represented them under all sorts of labels ranging from extreme right to extreme left.

The most striking phenomenon in twentieth-century France was that, whereas the fundamental division of interests (apart from class warfare) was between the industrial and urban population on the one hand and the rural population on the other there was not in any French parliament a single party which represented the peasantry. There was a sprinkling of agrarians in assorted groups, such, for instance, as the 'Parti Ouvrier et Paysan', but those were militant revolutionaries voicing some specific claims, and not delegates of a large section of the community.

The reason given for a distribution of parties which was not connected with any tangible realities was that a large agrarian movement in France could only have widened the gap between town and country. In practice, however, this gap existed all the same and the only effect of inadequate representation was to add confusion to differences. These remained unsolved, but hidden behind various smoke-screens. Such was the result of a party system based on historical memories rather than on hard economic facts.

Every political group attempted to secure the support of both industry and peasantry. This led to dogmatic jugglery at every turn. Thus, the S.F.I.O. Socialists,[1] who took their gospel from Marx, had to preach the abolition of private property amongst industrial workers. Yet having an eye on rural votes they could not go the whole hog. Some Socialist exponents eventually found a way out by stating that the right to 'small property' was justifiable, but that it should be limited. The believers were left to transcribe this Delphic oracle into shillings and pence, or, rather, francs and sous.

Conversely, the peasants who were not represented as such in parliament, had occasionally, in order to voice their claims, to resort to politicians whose opinions were radically different from their own. In most respects the peasantry was conservative. But if the candidates of its own persuasion lacked stamina or forcefulness in the advocacy of its interests, it would not hesitate to enlist champions in the other camp. Such political illogicalities were frequent after the turn of the 'thirties. The precedent was set in 1929. Léon Blum, the leader of the S.F.I.O. party, was out of parliament. He was needed to lead the opposition against the Conservative government. A seat was vacant in Narbonne, a region of wine-growers and well-to-do agriculturalists, passionately attached to their land-holdings. In those days, Léon Blum was an outspoken collectivist in the best orthodox tradition, and recruited his natural clientèle among the industrial proletariat. Yet he was a very distinguished orator and Narbonne wanted an outstanding champion. He was elected. In exchange, Léon Blum, a Marxist, was expected to support claims relating to the sale of wine at remunerative prices and to their protection against Empire competition. Thus, a proletarian leader

[1] Section Française de l'Internationale Ouvrière, the orthodox Socialist Party.

was elected by small landowners. A collectivist was chosen to defend the keeping up of prices which made the consumption of wine more expensive for wage-earners. A progressive internationalist was asked to advocate economic protection.

Generally speaking, there were in France two sets of social problems. The first, with its inherent potentialities in terms of class war, was the status of the industrial proletariat never defined by an adequate charter. There was in the second place, the fundamental economic conflict between the interests of the peasantry and those of most other sections of the nation. This proceeded from the basic contest with regard to prices as between producers and consumers. On ethical and social grounds, it was intensified by different conceptions of life. The peasants remained conservative, attached to local customs, and organizations. They were prudent in foreign policy. The industrial and maritime population disliked any form of regionalism, encouraged centralization, and was on the whole more adventurous in international affairs. As between the two sections, the tradition of the Revolution, kept alive by most parties, provided a lowest common denominator of dubious practical value.

The peasantry sceptically picked up its representatives according to opportunity and specific requirements. (Whilst there existed in fact French thinkers and economists who considered its problems in their true light and perspective, these men, unfortunately, were kept or kept themselves away from the political arena.) The town workmen adopted a less philosophical attitude. From the Amsterdam Conference in 1905 they supported the Socialist party which hailed from the French Revolution in ethics but from Marxism in politics and on social issues, making praiseworthy efforts to reconcile these divergent principles. After the Great War (at the Party Conference of Tours in 1922) the French section of the Second International split into two parts, the orthodox Socialists and the Communists. The latter became the French section of the Third International, taking its catechism from the Russian Revolution.

It must be remembered that it was only in 1932 that working-class representation became sufficiently weighty in the French parliament to secure any tangible reforms. Until that time progress in social legislation had been slow and sporadic. Even the Left governments, like the 'Cartel des Gauches' of 1924, had been composite combinations ruled by the Radicals whose allegiance was strongly divided between industrial workers and peasantry and whose programme was closer than any other to the 1789 tradition—especially in its vagueness.

Although in 1932 the Radicals were still the dominant party, the influence of the Socialists made itself felt to a degree hitherto unknown. By then, the French social problem, already complex enough, had been aggravated still further by the intervention of a new factor, the spreading into France of foreign ideologies.

Traditional divisions between 'blacks' and 'reds' became more acute through economic difficulties in the twentieth century and class warfare born of industrial evolution and legislative inadequacy. They received stimulus from foreign ideologies which, at the same time, complicated every issue, infected every group, and confused the French picture to such an extent that it rendered national problems almost unrecognizable in a welter of notions, ideas, traditions, prejudices, slogans, and 'isms' of all sorts. Communism in a form which was utterly unadaptable to French economy had been introduced into France at the end of the last war and had received its charter at the Tours Conference. For ten years it was only represented by a small parliamentary group. Although the party did not reach its full stature until 1936, its membership began to grow in the early 'thirties. During the same epoch and perhaps as a reaction against the advance of the extreme Left, sundry tendencies of markedly foreign origin found their way into France. The country harboured at the time three million aliens who had either acquired French nationality or, in their foreign capacity, enjoyed the same rights as French citizens.[1] The political arena in France was free for all and became a playground for alien ideologies.

Repeatedly, throughout French history, foreign influences had reached France and occasionally made themselves felt in an active way. Culturally, they had always been an asset. Politically, they were harmless enough when they only penetrated a highly cultured community. In that case they were even profitable. Thus in the eighteenth century the merits of British parliamentary institutions had been truly gauged and appreciated by the French Encyclopedists, who had evolved, from

[1] This figure in 1939 reached the fantastic total of nearly five millions. When war broke out all foreigners in France had enjoyed for twenty years rights and freedom absolutely unparalleled and unprecedented in any other country. No other nation has ever shown such hospitality and toleration. Yet to-day France is sometimes judged merely on those rigorous measures which she had to take under stress in the late 'thirties. Some of those who had found in her a last refuge, thrived on her, and even abused her hospitality by fanning or even provoking social unrest, are, of course, among the first to decry a nation without which they would have led the life of wandering and destitute pariahs, for emigration elsewhere was a mere trickle and demanded sterner guarantees.

the study of them, principles of political reform adaptable to
their own country.

These influences in the early 'thirties invaded France bru-
tally, irrationally, and indiscriminately. They were propagated
either by Frenchmen who sought in alien régimes new patterns for France, or directly and outspokenly by foreign elements who were interested parties. Gradually, various forms
of communism, Italian corporativism and, later, even German
national-socialism found in France advocates, heralds, and
agents who were not always benevolent. Absorbed without
assimilation these dogmas from abroad were swallowed, hook,
line, and sinker, by irresponsible groups, most of which did
not realize at first that they might be political weapons in the
hands of foreign powers.

The first attempts made by a Left government in 1932 to
introduce some measure of social legislation released political
aspirations on the one hand and political passions on the other.
In social legislation, France was definitely deficient. The appe-
tites of progressive and revolutionary groups were naturally
whetted by the prospect of a substantial advance in this field.
The privileged classes had grown accustomed to the idea that,
like sea-captains on their ships, they were in their own concerns the sole masters after God. From the outset, their resistance was fierce. The class problem thus clearly raised might
have been solved on purely national bases. It was soon em-
bittered by the rise of extra-parliamentary groups which,
under nationalistic or revolutionary labels, were in fact actively
importing into France slogans and methods borrowed from
other countries. The serious character of these foreign inspirations, however sincere their French promoters may have
been, was demonstrated on the 6th February 1934 on the Place
de la Concorde when, for the first time in sixty years, Paris
became the scene of riots which threatened to turn into civil
war. The most striking feature of this tragic incident was that
most of the groups and factions which played a leading part
in its engineering were, in the traditional sense of the word,
equally non-French in their political conceptions.

The 6th February, which caused the 'abdication' of M.
Daladier's Left-wing government, was followed by an apparent swing to the Right: only apparent, however, because,
whilst the opponents of social reform gained the upper hand
in government circles, theirs proved to be a short-lived victory. Social evolution continued. It had been denied recognition, but could not be reversed. In this respect, the governments which followed the 6th February succeeded only in
embittering the working class. At the same time, as they were

giving official countenance to the reactionary instincts of French employers, the class problem could only rankle. Nor was the economic issue as between the peasantry and the industrial population seriously considered and coped with. Moreover, the groups formed partly by sincere patriots and partly by admirers of foreign régimes grew into factions under the indulgent eyes of the central authority. The reaction to these, as well as to the failure of the first Left-wing government, which had disappointed many hopes, took the form of an increase in the membership of the Communist Party. For both the extreme Right and the extreme Left, the French parliament had ceased to be an adequate platform for the ventilation of claims and grievances. There was a marked tendency to resort to street demonstrations if not to direct action. Amid the clamour of new-fangled political movements, it was not easy to distinguish the true national voice and the true French accent.

It was the Spanish Civil War which made the deepest rent in French social life. By then, the general elections of 1936 had returned a parliamentary majority which gave France her second markedly left-wing Government, best remembered as the 'Popular Front'. The Spanish war produced in France the most striking example of social strife combining and confusing the three main factors of internal dissension: class warfare, 'black' and 'red' antagonism, foreign ideologies. It touched every nerve, rubbed and reopened every wound. It widened the gap between proletariat and capitalist, anti-clerical progressive and catholic conservative, the sympathizer with Russia and the exponent of totalitarianism. In her profound, vehement reaction to the Spanish war, France showed what a crucial point she had reached in her historical evolution and in the tragedy caused by the upset of her economic and social balance.

It is often asserted that such and such a politician or party was responsible for the social strife which saddened the last years of the Third Republic. It is true that after the death of the old guard France did not produce outstanding statesmen. The last war had maimed the best part of those generations that should have supplied the successors to the great leaders who had governed the French people between the end of the last century and the late 'twenties.

It may be wondered, however, whether the problem could have been solved within less than twenty years by methods which democratic statesmen were entitled to apply. Demographically, economically, and socially the transformation which France needed to adapt herself to European conditions in terms of power would have demanded truly revolutionary methods.

Apart from human shortcomings there is in every crisis an element of fate. France's demographic means had been reduced by the last war and her economic dualism had prevented any lasting equilibrium—the condition essential to a rise in the birthrate. This dualism could not be resolved without profound social disturbances. As it was, it had maintained France in the position of a country whose industrial equipment was out of proportion to her traditional role in the face of an enemy who drew his striking power from a revolutionary economic process. Her dualism had also prolonged into the twentieth century a social balance which, ideal in the past, became precarious in the modern world. Finally her sensitiveness to European influences had turned into a liability when the ideological weapon was used against her social life. Nothing short of a revolution—granting it sufficient far-sightedness—could have reversed the stream. Yet it is rare to find in a victorious nation men who dare enforce drastic changes to provide against incalculable events. Hitler might have been stopped in time. Hitler's achievements in terms of physical power could not have been foreseen.

Given the individual qualities of the French people, the true balance would have been found. These qualities had not been impaired, but when France had to fulfil her international task she had been for seven years undergoing a deep and painful process of evolution. More precisely, she had lived in a state of endemic revolution. International events making themselves felt throughout the country had hidden its national sense, which ran like an unseen current under the ripples.

Party governments were inadequate to cope with the basic issues (not because Party government is not desirable in itself but because parties in France were both out of date and far too numerous). They were confronted with the problems of a lifetime which they had to solve sporadically in time and space. Each partial settlement in favour of a given group led to discontent elsewhere, so long as these problems were not tackled at their roots. A typical government puzzle was this: Wages were insufficient in a certain industry. They could not be substantially raised because production was not standardized and remunerative. This was due to lack of industrial concentration as compared with other countries which could afford higher wages whilst maintaining reasonable prices. An alternative solution to higher wages is, of course, a reduction in the prices of staple commodities. These were produced in France on an uneconomic basis because the land had to provide

remuneration for a rural population in excess of strict requirements. Finally, the only palliative took the shape of subsidies
in both directions and of a new burden on the Treasury.
England has also known her 'vicious spiral', but with two
capital qualifications: the manipulation of prices was conceivable in England without affecting a peasantry representing half
the population of the country; the social problem in Great
Britain remained isolated from direct European currents.

To the outside world the French social problem in the years
which preceded the present war appeared to be merely the
result of political bickerings growing into ideological feuds.
In fact the deep causes were truly economic, but then the
French are seldom capable of considering a collective economic issue in purely economic terms. Save within the orbit of
the family they are not economically minded! On the other
hand they are politically highly strung; a legacy from the days
when the great state problem in France lay in preventing
wars from endangering her natural and coveted wealth and in
collecting taxes from more or less reluctant tax-payers. In
recent times, this political susceptibility, galled by the recur-
rence of social or economic problems left unsolved and fanned
by new ideological slogans, gave to French public life a
character of chronic agitation. The existence of political parties which were out of touch with contemporary realities,
because they had sprung from dead tradition rather than living
necessity, contributed to political instability. Political programmes were framed in mysterious phraseology borrowed
from such past controversies as the Dreyfus Case: the result
was that parliamentary institutions fell into disrepute, and
irresponsible factions which took to direct action on behalf of
national ideals found some popular support and had time to
do considerable damage before they began to decline.

Meanwhile every German had been turned into a cog in the
war machine. Hitler's was a Power Revolution: not a social one

CHAPTER VIII

INTELLECTUAL AND MORAL HAMLETISM

IN 1927, Julien Benda, in a book entitled *The Treason of the
Learned*,[1] raised the fundamental issue of the social function of literature. Put briefly, the treason of the learned

[1] *La trahison des clercs.* English translation by Richard Aldington,
The Great Betrayal (London, 1928).

G

was their divorce from the French tradition of intellectual moralism. In Benda's opinion French literature and ethics had lost sight of their true human purpose, which is and must remain the study of man. The conception of man as part of a political evolution had taken precedence over that of man as a human entity.

This phenomenon was of course partly due to the Romantic legacy. Throughout the nineteenth century, general literature, including essays and even poetry, had invaded the political and social arena and often deserted the traditional object of art in France, which was the scrutiny, statement, and representation of man's individual motives and passions. The process of interference with collective evolution and social change was, if anything, accelerated during the twentieth century, especially in the years which followed the first World War.

It was therefore inevitable that literature and art should reflect the conflict of tendencies and aspirations which marked this period. Against this form of 'interventionism' Benda urged the learned to return to their historical pursuits, which in his opinion should remain the essential ones. Ethical and artistic thought must, according to him, stand as a steady guide, 'constant as the Northern Star'. Interest in political problems must not eclipse the basic concern with human nature as such. His effort received due praise, but his remained a *vox clamans in deserto*. Apart from the cheaper varieties of literary production, most French writers still kept their eyes on the social and political target. Thus it happened that in most cases novelists, essayists, playwrights were caught in the storms of popular feeling and passion.

Of these years it has been said that they were rich in talent and very poor in genius. A French humorist came close to the truth when he remarked during the late 'twenties: 'This a post-war period? In literary genres, it is a pre-war period. They all look as though they were expecting something to happen or fearing to lose those things they hold dear. They are all either waiting or remembering.' And, indeed, many writers were 'remembering' and salvaging material from the past. If one wished to indulge the habit of arbitrary classification, such names might be singled out as those of Estaunié, Régnier, Paul Bourget (Bourget of whom it was said that he took no interest in psychological subjects unless they could boast of a five-figure income), Colette, and even younger authors ranging from Cocteau to Sarment and Claude Anet. Others were 'waiting', and a note of expectancy or mutability rang through their works: André Gide (although he belonged to a pre-war world), Duhamel, Montherlant, Giono

VI.
PEACEFUL
FRANCE

1. HARVESTING
(*Margot Lubinski*)

2. LACEMAKING
(*Margot Lubinski*)

Green, Céline. Others were trying to assess lasting values threatened with oblivion, either as one draws up a balance sheet before a liquidation or in order to give some fixity to those things which might survive: Paul Claudel, Mauriac, Bernanos, Maritain, and, in a different realm, Henri Pourrat. Then there were the adventurous escapists seeking diversion in action: Cendrars, MacOrlan, Morand, Miomandre, Saint-Exupéry (although in the case of the latter, action was a means to an end: the rehabilitation of character).

Few were the works which did not betray a sense of impermanence and of radical change. In 1925 a young French writer, Daniel Rops, produced an essay more notable for its title and object than for its substance. The title was *Notre Inquiétude* (in the sense of moral unrest rather than anxiety). Daniel Rops attempted to define a state of mind born of the war: a sort of replica of the German *Sturm und Drang*. The author described how the Great War had broken the sense of continuity in general ethics and how difficult it became to find values which had stood through the storm and could still provide a bedrock on which to build.

What had in fact been lost was the sense of national tradition. It had been lost in two respects: first because literature and art had forgotten their true purpose, which was the moral scrutiny of man; and secondly because in their political pursuits they had undergone a process of denationalization. Indeed, in terms of ethics, the most challenged of all values in the years which followed the first World War was precisely the national one. It was assailed from every quarter. Apart from such signal exceptions as Paul Claudel, or open advocates of political nationalism such as Charles Maurras, the national tradition was upheld in literature chiefly by a set of deserted Academicians who served it ill by clinging to obsolete shibboleths and prejudices. Through the statesmen and politicians of the old school, the national tradition found utterance in international conferences, but it hardly did so in French thought and literature. During the second post-war Poincaré government, Gaston Riou had written a book called *Europe, ma Patrie* and dedicated it to Raymond Poincaré. This statesman who read everything (the Germans complained that he even ran through every paragraph of their second-rate provincial rags), thanked him for his dedication but remarked to him in public: 'Europe is all very well, but you should remember that your motherland is France and that Europe only comes second.' Polemists of all descriptions swooped upon this reply which brought forth a crop of scathing articles on Poincaré's narrow-mindedness. Nationalism was not in fashion during the 'twenties amongst the majority of French writers and controversialists. They were inclined to find their ethical *raison d'être* either in a wider concept such as Europe, or in internationalistic dogmas, or even in individualistic nihilism. There were few members of the younger generation who had not read Kropotkin and occasionally dreamt of such an anarchistic community as the 'Clock-makers' of the Jura as an anticipation of a future and better world. One of the reactions to victory was a fever of intellectual denationalization. Had not the elder statesmen of the last war been backed in those days by the conservative peasantry and the *bourgeoisie* (for internal rather than for external reasons), the youth and intellectual *élite* of France would probably have reversed what remained for over ten years the foreign policy of France.

Foreign influences, which had always been welcome in France and had constantly brought an influx of suggestions and thought, were snatched with such avidity as to confuse and complicate the French cultural picture to the utmost, adding to the confusion by introducing into that realm alien political inspirations. Whether it was expressed by Malraux, a good and true writer, or by Emmanuel Berl, a semi-agitator, such a notion as Permanent Revolution (Revolution as an end in itself, as a permanent stimulus and not as a means of securing definite reforms) was not and could not be a part of the French mental make-up. Yet this concept remained in vogue for some years amongst an important section of the young French *intelligentsia*.

It is true that the foremost French writers did not wholly participate in this orgy of national self-denial. Paul Valéry, Gide, Giraudoux (already shining out by the side of older glories), Mauriac, Lacretelle, Duhamel, Romains, Colette, retained a sense of proportion. But few of them, tempted by a broader and more generous conception of the world, had not occasionally come to question national values. In 1930 Valéry gave Marshal Pétain a lesson in European-mindedness as tactfully impertinent in its delicate irony as circumstances permitted (he was receiving the old Marshal at the French Academy). Giraudoux in *Bella* had made an incisive satire of 'Poincarism'. Gide at sixty turned to Communism, only to recant a few years later. Duhamel had shown the vanity of national wars in *Civilisation* and left in his *Salavins* a lasting picture of the inevitable conflict between man and his social environment. Even Mauriac, traditionalist though he was, did not prove altogether constructive, nor did he offer solid values to which one could cling.

Essayists and other writers had stepped into the arena of

political and social controversy. Naturally they expounded
and amplified the problems of conscience, the conflicting tendencies and the differences of those whom they intended to
educate. Instead of guides they became intellectual 'militants'.
This turned out to be the consequence of the Treason of the
Learned: having partly abandoned their true pursuits and
deserted their own paths in order to take an active share in the
guidance of 'the masses', they merely reflected in an intelligible but unhelpful way the changing moods and variable influences of their time. Or, alternatively, some of them would
take refuge from the battlefield in an 'ivory tower' from which
they uttered pronouncements hardly accessible to the general
public.

It is difficult to refer to the 'twenties without mentioning
the Surrealist movement, whose literary promoter in France
was Guillaume Appollinaire, a true and original poet, and
whose followers were Aragon, Breton, and Tristan Tzara.
This movement, which sought inspiration not in rational
thought and processes of logical analysis, but in the suggestive
qualities of words, sounds, or images, may well be considered
as the unconscious prophet of things to come: the omen of a
European reshuffle, and of an utter loss of connexion between
European values, of a time when every accepted belief would
be thrown into the melting-pot.

After the turn of the 'twenties, there was some return to
discipline of thought. Incidentally, a second-rate book by
Marcel Arlan which received the Prix Goncourt may be chosen
at random as a symptom of this reaction. Its title was significant, *L'Ordre*. The reaction manifested itself in two ways.
Politically, national values resumed their place. Ethically,
man, as a living individual, irrespective of time and space,
became once more the object of study. There was even a
suggestion of pure classicism in style and thought. An outstanding writer and dramatist like Giraudoux truly restored
the human problem to its proper ground.

This reaction did not last for long, and was, in any case, no
more than partial. The weight of social evolution and of
extraneous influences upon French literature and art was
crushing during the five or six years which preceded the second
World War. A school whose ambitions were generous, the
'Populistes', appeared claiming to be the literary interpreter
of the masses. It was in fact a resurrection of Zola with a ven-
geance. French advocates of foreign régimes and ideologies
used the literary weapon for political purposes. They occasionally acted under the mantle of the 'Populistes'. A striking
instance of this was Louis-Ferdinand Céline who hailed from

the people and even used with some distinction a style borrowed from slang, eventually to fall a prey to downright hitlerism, which he propagated in France.

Other writers made themselves the champions of individualism, but in a way which bore the stamp of an alien philosophy.
Their individualism was not, according to the French tradition, a clear, rational conception of the human person. It was
an exuberant form of self-assertion, of individual self-exalta-
tion, a kind of French Nietzscheism. The latest novels by
Montherlant provide a very clear illustration of this tendency,
which was sarcastically described by one of Montherlant's
detractors as 'muscular metaphysics'.

In all this, there was a wealth of talent. French style, French
gifts of presentation, were still there. But instead of remaining
a cultural clearing-house for Europe, France had gradually
become an amplifier of manifold and conflicting ideas, some
of them originating in her own social unrest, some of them in
aspirations peculiar to other countries undergoing similar processes, most of them lacking cohesion. The centre of gravity
was not always in France, and the French touchstone was
hardly applied with discrimination.

With regard to the more popular forms of art, such as the
cinema, or journalism, which is, after all, the most accessible
form of literature, these, in terms of intellectual value, if
not on technical merits, afforded little comfort and still less
guidance. The cinema is perhaps the only art which does not
lose through being no more than a mirror of contemporary
events or preoccupations. Yet, for all its richness, the French
film never offered examples of a production as substantial and
illustrative of contemporary human problems as the American
Grapes of Wrath or Chaplin's *Modern Times*. What can be
said of other forms of art also applies to the cinema. Abroad,
it was recognized as French for its merits in craftsmanship,
lighting, and wit. In France itself, such achievements were
taken for granted and one looked in vain for a more substantial
contribution. The wide popular appeal of foreign films in
France suffices in itself to indicate the inadequacy of the
French product in this respect, though French hopes were
often disappointed even there.

In the minor literary forms, if journalism and pamphlets can
so be described, the true sense of national responsibility had
been lost. Newspapers and pamphlets merely transcribed the
fluctuations of political life. It looked as though politics had
ceased to relate to the government of men and had become a
stage for exhibitions exposed for free criticism, with this
reservation—that the rules of common courtesy were applied

to the stage, while politicians were less favoured. Behind the reputable journalists there grew a crop of others who permanently ruined the reputation of the press: most of their names have, incidentally, reappeared among the exponents of collaboration with Germany. Any country, of course, produces a certain number of common crooks. If these could thrive in France and play a political part, it was made possible by the lack of solid values and tangible articles of faith which characterizes a period of social evolution and unrest.

The same applies to the famous scandals of the Third Republic: those of Roquette, Hanau, Stavisky. The main tragedy was not that certain people should be in the dock, but that the public should wonder whether the accusers should not themselves have been in the dock too. Parliamentary institutions had ceased to be respected because they did not tackle the basic problems set France by her economic situation. Once respect and confidence have been lost in the relationship between a people and its representatives, scepticism and indifference stimulate the least creditable members of the community and encourage them to exploit the advantages of the position. Corruption becomes possible. Yet scandals and even corruption, the extent of which was exaggerated by public discontent and by the French passion for generalization, would have remained episodic and subordinate if the very bases of the French national life had not been seriously shaken. Scepticism, disbelief, instability of outlook, are more far-reaching diseases than offences against a common code. For they make it possible to commit these offences with impunity. Any community will supply an assortment of Staviskys, but a healthy nation will break them.

The loss of a sense of balance inevitably causes a return to individual rules and self-chosen standards of behaviour as against collective codes. During the past twenty years, the vast majority of French citizens were still profoundly attached to moral values in their private pursuits, but they felt them to be far less binding in public life.

Apart from the intellectual *élites* and political leaders, there still subsisted in France during those twenty years a considerable force which could have played its part in maintaining coherence and order in community life, and enforced common allegiance to ethical standards: the Roman Catholic Church. Yet even in that 'sanctuary of calm and serenity', standing aloof amid contentious factions, the great unrest in moral and spiritual life which was born of the war could not fail to have its echoes. They were discreet and muffled, but, still, they were heard. The Church of St. Peter is, by definition, the widest and most ancient international body in the world. More than temporal organizations, it must keep contact with European currents and cross-currents and with those expressions of the aspirations and passions of men: wars, upheavals, revolutions. On a higher plane the Church partook of the moral crisis of France. It also had its problems of conscience. Ripples appeared on the calm waters. The Church realized, after the first World War, that the forces which the conflict had released throughout France and Europe would be neither curbed nor assuaged by exhortations addressed merely to the individual conscience in the darkness of the confessional. The believers might look to the Church for a refuge or perhaps an occasional respite from temporal cares and turmoil. But the Church might find it difficult to weigh on the side of social and moral order merely by virtue of its teachings. Should it still retain its character as a spiritual force above temporal storms, in order to rebuild and heal, once those storms had blown over or even done their work of destruction? or should it, in so far as its high standards permitted, descend into the arena?

The problem was more serious than at any previous time in history. In most countries, the Catholic Church had been disestablished. Then, in the twentieth century, temporal powers had resorted to ideological weapons and introduced confusion into the human conscience as to the respective attributes of the State and the Church. They trespassed on its realm. They took a leaf from its book. Between ideological values defended and glorified with mystical fervour by temporal rulers on the one hand and religious faith on the other, the margin was increasingly narrow. At any time, men imbued with the former might forget the latter. Moreover, where political or ideological passion ceased to be a danger, scepticism born from national or social disillusionment might extend its destructive influence to the very articles of faith which the Church must uphold. Such were the arguments in favour of 'intervention'.

The case for non-interference was equally strong. By fighting its own battle, the Church might lose its most precious asset: its value as a refuge, as a judge in the last resort, and as a guide when all else failed. Moreover, the Church cannot take sides. It is non-national. In matters of faith, what is truth in Rome is truth in Paris. But in politics, truth in Rome is usually falsehood in Paris. Intervention might lead to religious schism after six hundred years of unity.

This religious 'to be or not to be' remained without an official answer. In practice, the Church moved towards a compromise. It did not take any open political action. But it allowed social organizations to seek inspiration in its bosom. It showed a growing interest in problems of social welfare on a wider scale than the traditional duty of charity demanded. Shortly before the present war, its influence was beginning to make itself felt very noticeably, and a sound programme reconciling social progress with spiritual values was gradually unfolding itself. Such organizations as the 'Jeunesses Ouvrières Chrétiens' and 'Jeunesses Agricoles Chrétiennes' were remarkable steps forward. Moreover, they might have provided a cement between those two sections of the French population whose antagonism remained a serious aspect of the social problem in France: the industrial and the agricultural populations. This healthy process of evolution was unfortunately interrupted by the war, but it may well provide a valuable precedent for future reformers.

To some issues which aroused vehement feelings in the French masses, the Church found it difficult to supply an answer. Against those and their effects, the Church itself was not always proof. During the Spanish war, for instance, there was a noticeable difference of opinion between the higher clergy and the lower, the former inclining to support the Whites, and numbers of the latter feeling more sympathetic towards the Republicans. For some time the great social dissensions of the twentieth century appeared to threaten even religious unity. A fervent Catholic writer, Georges Bernanos, challenged the orthodox view by publishing a mighty and scathing indictment of the Whites and their clerical supporters in *Les Grands Cimetières sous la Lune*, in which he asserted that the so-called defenders of order and faith were trampling the teachings of Christ.

On the whole, the Church remained a strong influence in France, but it occasionally found it difficult to bring its full weight to bear on the side of moral unity. But some of its initiatives in the social field certainly represented a measure of advance towards both social progress and order.

In 1939, all the *élite*, spiritual or temporal, rallied to the national cause. They did it with unanimous conviction, without hesitation or mental reservation. Yet too many men had been late in their intellectual or ethical 'rearmament'. 'The native hue of resolution' had been dangerously 'sicklied o'er with the pale cast of thought', and the thought had not always been of purely national inspiration.

CHAPTER IX

THE FRENCH DEFEAT

WHEN France went to war she was not in a position to withstand the German impact by her own means: and this for demographic, economic, and social reasons. She had in all these respects to resume her balance or to find a new one under twentieth-century conditions. To use a convenient comparison, she was, as a result of her process of evolution, like a tennis player caught on the wrong foot. Such an accident is not without precedents either in her own history or that of other countries. But the geographical situation of France did not permit her to resort to the expedient usual in such cases, that of gaining time.

It is clear that Hitler had fully realized the state of transformation and endemic revolution of France and other European nations. His repeated statement that he 'would rather go to war at fifty than at fifty-five' meant more than that he wanted to lead his country to war before age overcame him. Hitler's revolution in his own country had not been a social reformation but a social, economic, and spiritual rearmament. He had rallied in Germany all the elements which for centuries had been potential factors of war, and eliminated by coercive methods all those which showed static, conservative, or sceptical dispositions. That was the sum total of his revolution. The glorification of the blood-tie, the curbing of the Church, the persecution of the Jews, the destruction of all forms of opposition to a war drive: all this no more amounts to a revolution than Hitler's financial and fiscal methods, which boil down to a gigantic mortgage on future conquests (as witness Schacht's present scheme, by which he turns German indebtedness into French long-term inflation). Hitler made his revolution for war purposes, with the deliberate object of postponing the real issue until he had achieved victory. Racially, socially, and economically his revolution was merely a ruthless form of mobilization.

In other countries, the evolutionary process was normal and therefore slower. In terms of power, European nations were affected by it, but Hitler knew that these nations, and France in particular, would eventually resume their balance. He must therefore go to war at fifty rather than at fifty-five because in a few years his own revolution would have ended in a fiasco, whilst other States would have regained their poise. There again, his main fear was Russia, whose régime seemed more watertight than any other and less vulnerable to the weapon of social propaganda, although Hitler entertained the hope that there might by now be some cracks in the Russian edifice.

In the case of France, his calculation of 'timing' was correct. In 1939 the various elements of the French crisis had lost their virulence but the effects of the crisis had endured. The French body was more vulnerable. It had not entirely recuperated. Time had been too short.

The French people went to war serious and determined but without flowers and songs. Every one sensed that France had to fulfil her traditional mission in unfavourable circumstances. It may be that military leaders underestimated the might of Germany. Instinctively, the people of France looked at the respective figures of population, remembered the tremendous efforts made by Germany for six years, and were inclined to scepticism when told that Germany's weapons were inadequate or that the Reich was deficient in trained reserves. In this, popular wisdom showed more perspicacity than the technicians.

In fact, if one looks back upon those tragic events of 1940 with a knowledge of actual data which only experience has supplied, the odds against the French nation were heavy indeed. It went to war with weapons considerably inferior to those of Germany in quantity and efficiency (in absolute quality, French tanks, for instance, were superior to their rivals in terms of wear and tear, and even armour; but in speed, which proved to be a determining factor, the Germans had the advantage). It went to war with a High Command and a body of permanent regimental officers who were either too old or too young, because of the rent made in French manhood by the last war, and who soon became conscious of the odds against them. It went to war with a civil administration which had been found out of date and was undermined by social feuds or local politics (as the defeatism of some *préfets* after the first reverses was to demonstrate). It went to war in a state of tremendous numerical inferiority, and could not expect this inferiority to be offset even at a later stage. In fact, as against the last war, only one source of strength remained unimpaired in spite of all: the aptitude of the individual Frenchman to defend his soil and his readiness to accept the full sacrifice. The last stages of the campaign cannot disprove this statement: when an army is broken the individual resources of its soldiers can play little part in modern warfare.

Much has been said and still more written on the strategic attitude (for it was more an attitude than a true strategy), contemptuously described as 'Maginot-mindedness'. The problem cannot be dismissed as lightly as it often has been.

Inferiority in numbers, in war material, and generally in means of manœuvring, made a policy of strategic initiative extremely hazardous. Should the initiative fail, the effects would be catastrophic. The Maginot policy was founded on the assumption that, whatever happened, the French army could defend its territory, but that its ability to take the offensive was more than doubtful. Whether this argument is fundamentally correct or not, remains open to question. But it still awaits a rational answer. If the French, passionately attached as they are to their land, were unable to withstand the German onslaught, it is difficult to imagine how the disabilities under which they had to fight, through lack of proper leadership and other deficiencies, could suddenly have been turned into assets by the mere process of launching a general offensive.

Pending further information, common sense seems to suggest that the main drawback of the Maginot policy was the lack of a Maginot line. There was an excellent system of fortifications from the Swiss frontier down to Longwy. It proved its worth by resisting several days after the conclusion of the armistice, when it was completely surrounded. But along a stretch of nearly 300 miles, the Maginot line was conspicuous by its absence.

What has been clearly shown by experience is not the error of the Maginot policy (although it may well be that this will be clearly demonstrated at some future time), but the absurdity of a strategy which was based on defence, which created among the French people a psychosis of defence, and which yet neglected an obvious and wide route of invasion. This, above everything else, is the proven mistake of the French High Command. It is not proposed here to pass judgement on purely military problems, nor am I qualified for the task. But such a gross inconsistency in strategy is a challenge to common sense. For the fact that France was not from the outset in a position to show off brilliantly, the first World War, the French national crisis, and the lack of substantial military help from abroad, would have accounted. Until such time as the Allies had marshalled their strength, at least an inglorious policy of wait and see could have been adopted on the Western front—not excluding initiatives elsewhere. But what is blatantly absurd on any ground is to base a war strategy on the notion of initial inferiority, to evolve a strategy of defence on these premisses, and then to neglect the most elementary precautions.

The excuse sometimes offered is that adequate fortifications on the frontiers of Luxemburg and Belgium might have

offended the Belgian Government. As Belgium never agreed
to co-ordinate her own strategy with that of the French, save
at the last minute, it is difficult to see how the Belgian government could have taken exception to elementary measures of
self-defence. Moreover, on national grounds, such an argument is unacceptable. A great Power cannot be expected to
run the risk of being wiped out for fear of hurting even a
friend's feelings.

It is not only in the organization of French defences that
the policy of the High Command glaringly contradicted itself.
Having banked on defence and lulled its army into a defensive
attitude for over eight months, it eventually launched that same
army into Belgium on the 10th May 1940. The fact that
French and British troops were going out to meet the German
offensive does not alter the terms of the problem, nor does it
affect the illogicality of its solution. If conditions made a
policy of defence imperative and prevented the French from
taking the initiative even at the time when the Germans were
encountering the heroic resistance of the Poles, the sudden
return to a strategy of movement after the Germans had taken
the lead and chosen both time and ground for striking in conditions determined by themselves, could hardly turn out to be
a successful venture. It was all the more so since the consulta-
tions with France's new ally, Belgium, had been negligible.
Whether public and even world opinion demanded that such
a move into Belgium should be made, is wholly irrelevant to
the point. A High Command has to take stock of a situation
and stick to its guns. In the event, Belgium came under
German occupation and so did France.

The fact is that the Germans were attacking with a completely unified body of men, in huge numbers, and with formidable material which incidentally proved, in respect of
tanks, to be twice as strong as the French High Command had
estimated. The French were going into Belgium to meet the
enemy, at the enemy's own time, with inferior numbers, armaments, and staff, and with armies whose co-ordination with
their Belgian allies had been improvised in a little less than
a week.

The result was that the French High Command was completely outmanœuvred. Conceived in terms of academic warfare, the French plan to meet the contingency of a German
attack through Belgium was masterly; but undoubtedly the
Germans were aware of it, and found it easy to forestall and
stultify the proposed operations.

The lack of co-ordination and the consequent miscalculation of strategic possibilities were exemplified when the French

High Command discovered that the Albert Canal had been forced in less than forty-eight hours, though on the strength of Belgian calculations they had expected it to hold for several days. The disadvantage of fighting with inferior resources on a ground and at a time chosen by the enemy was strikingly demonstrated when the Germans directed their main thrust against Sedan, at the very hinge of the Allied front, which the French High Command had indifferently protected. It was believed at the time that the German forces only succeeded in piercing the French lines because the bridges on the Meuse had not been blown up. This allegation has recently been refuted. With or without bridges, the German army would have gone through. The ground had been well reconnoitred, the plans well laid. The Germans, and more recently the Japanese, have shown that rivers are not insuperable obstacles. What is quite clear is that the French High Command, having adopted a passive attitude for over eight months, abandoned its policy in circumstances which not only did not warrant a hope of success but could hardly have been more unfavourable.

At the time of the German offensive in the Low Countries, the French aircraft and tank factories were at last beginning to produce a substantial output. If ever the policy of gaining time might have been justified, it was certainly at the precise moment when the enemy offered to give battle on his own terms and when there was reasonable hope of an early increase in the physical means of resisting him. It may be that, even so, the unpreparedness of French defences on the north-west frontier would still have had fatal consequences. As it was, the results were catastrophic. The Allies lost some 50 per cent. of their man-power through the combined effects of the German encirclement and the Belgian capitulation.

Whether the 'Maginot strategy' was the only conceivable one at the time of the outbreak of war with the means available to the French High Command, must be left for future military historians to decide. The only truth which has emerged so far, from the evidence at hand, is not that this strategy was at fault, but that it was not followed to its logical conclusion either during the period described by the Americans as the 'phoney war' or after the German offensive. Had the Maginot line been prolonged to the sea, a frontal attack by the German armies would, to say the least, have resulted in considerable German losses: and that is, after all, the aim which the Russians pursued until such time as the Allies were able to take the offensive. In other words, a rational and comprehensive Maginot policy would have made the best of a fundamentally unsatisfactory situation.

Events since 1940 have by no means proved that a systematically offensive policy is profitable in all conceivable circumstances. They have merely confirmed the obvious truth that when chances are favourable for an offensive, the opportunity must be taken forthwith. It certainly does not prove that inferiority in numbers, leadership, and material is suddenly turned to advantage by the magic virtue of attack.

In 1939 and 1940 this inferiority existed and it was blatant.

When the dossier of these events is reopened in conditions ensuring complete objectivity, the case will have to be judged on grounds not of wishful thinking but of the unpleasant fact of France's inferiority. In the meantime it can certainly be said—irrespective of the intrinsic merits of the Maginot conception—that no clear line of policy was adopted and followed by the French High Command before the war, or during the war and after the German offensive. The same lack of planning and foresight was evident in its treatment of the problem set to France by the British alliance. There again, the High Command acted in complete contradiction of the very conceptions on which its strategy was based. It believed in defence because it was conscious of France's deficiencies. Yet it never brought home with sufficient force to the British government the fact that a large-scale participation in terms of man-power was more essential in this war than it had been in the last, since Germany had no second front in the East after the fall of Poland, and since the Belgian route of invasion lay as open in 1939 as in 1914. A limited participation on the part of Great Britain, in the military field, could only be contemplated on the basis of a strategy of fortifications. The openness of the Belgian route of invasion and the lack of fortifications on the north-west frontier did not allow the French General Staff to exclude the possibility of operations in the field. In fact these were probable, if not inevitable. In the field, the French army, which had to station troops on two other frontiers, would in any case have fought the Germans in conditions of considerable inferiority. Allied help was therefore more imperative in the present war than at any previous time. And it was the task of a Commander-in-Chief to assess his requirements and secure their fulfilment by Allied power. The British nation has shown since that it knew how to respond to a clear and true appeal. In 1939 the initiative for stating the case rested with the French High Command. The requirements were calculated on the basis of a policy of fortifications, which demanded the utilization of smaller forces, but this policy was never followed.

In this the French High Command not only minimized the German strength; it also displayed utter ignorance of the French soldiers' psychology. During the last war the French, in their struggle against the Central Powers, felt that the Western world was fighting by their side. In the present conflict, Germany was free from eastern entanglements. Her whole weight was concentrated on her Western walls. Two other French frontiers were threatened. And the French soldier was told by his High Command that, with a limited contribution from his British allies, he could easily tackle this tremendous task! The results of such an under-estimate of the peril could only be a feeling of unwarranted contempt for the enemy in some cases, a sentiment of moral solitude as time went on, and a state of bewilderment when the French army took full measure of the German might. In this the French High Command is also responsible for the temporary bitterness of the French soldiers towards their allies in June 1940. The French people had been misled, both in word and in deed.

Indeed, in this war, the French soldier was never given a fair chance. His individual and national qualities could play no part. Until the retreat on Dunkirk, the story was almost confined to a progressive disruption of the French military framework, in which men could show their fighting spirit only on occasions when they had to protect the rear of the evacuated armies.

In the second part of the campaign, after General Weygand had taken charge of the operations, the lines had been competently organized having regard to the means available. But the odds made resistance impossible for any length of time. With fifty-one divisions the French had to face over a hundred and fifty German divisions backed by a far superior equipment. For three days they held their front. When it was pierced at Forges-les-Eaux all hope of a successful resistance on metropolitan soil had to be abandoned. Within a week, there ceased to be any co-ordination between the various components of the French army. Army groups were fighting individually. And whilst the process of disintegration was accelerated on the French side, the German army was increasing in numbers. The civil administration was completely disrupted. The French army was soon reduced to a number of leaderless units whose chances of retrieving victory from chaos were non-existent, whose hopes of doing any serious damage to the enemy were slight, yet; contrary to a common impression, the amount of destruction wrought by French individual initiative was considerable.

H

Casual eye-witnesses who observed some of the scenes of
confusion which marked the last stages of the retreat, drew the
hasty conclusion that the individual French soldier had lost his
fighting qualities. Some severe judgements have been passed.
But war for a modern State depends for its conduct on a
tremendous military and administrative organization. Stamina,
spirit, resilience, on the part of the soldier can only assert
themselves within this framework. The army is a completely
hierarchized organism. When the nerve-centres and connect-
ing nerves have been crippled and disabled, the part played by
the limbs becomes negligible. Once anarchy succeeds order,
groups of brave men cannot make an army. There is, so far,
no example of armed resistance on a national scale, surviving
total disruption of authority and organization. Moreover,
modern civilized men do not fight for the sake of dying.
They fight to preserve something and according to a plan of
whose execution they are conscious. The French have a clear
notion of the object of their sacrifice. Utter self-denial they
accept out of enthusiasm or exaltation. But there is no such
stimulus in a complete defeat which strikes at the very roots
of belief and purpose. There was little stimulus, before the
defeat was irrevocable, in the spectacle of incompetence in the
preparation and in the political and strategic conduct of the
war. Where leaders were present and some remains of military cohesion apparent, the French soldiers fought even after
all hope had been abandoned. This was the case of the
Armée de l'Est, the best French army group, which for some
mysterious reason had been kept behind the fortifications of
the real Maginot line where it was least needed.

On the whole, a great number of Frenchmen, whether they
gave up or not, considered that the campaign of France had
been a tragic episode, but that the end of the Franco-German
tale had yet to be told. The memory of a long history of varying fortunes had convinced them that, whatever happened,
France would eventually survive and resume her rank in
Europe. By a strange paradox this inborn, instinctive faith in
the permanence of their country led many Frenchmen to
resign themselves to what they considered the inevitable.
They felt that the war had been waged and run with such
striking inefficiency from every quarter that they entertained
little hope of competent leadership on any other field of battle.
They did not know that England would fight on. When leadership reappeared and when England's stand proved that all hope
was not extinct, sufficient evidence was given that the fighting
qualities which in 1940 lacked both a cause and a point of
application were not eclipsed. The proof was given on many

a battlefield from Bir Hacheim to Tunis, from Tunis to Italy, and from Italy to France, on a scale, to be sure, which circumstances still limited—but proof enough, nevertheless, to re-assure the French people as to themselves and to restore confidence among their friends.

In June 1940 there was little to expect for the soldiers of an ill-used and defeated army. The French did not know that the last bulwark in the West would withstand the impact. They did not know that an army, small to begin with but which would steadily expand, would be raised out of the wreckage. Above all, they did not know themselves what untapped strength still lay in the prostrate body of their own nation—that within a very short space of time they themselves would resume the age-old struggle with Germany, although in a less active and glorious form: the resistance to German colonization and to 'collaboration'.

CHAPTER X

UNDER THE GERMAN HEEL

IT is imperative at this juncture to clarify an issue which has been clouded in propaganda and demagogic clichés: collaboration with Germany.

After the armistice many Englishmen were led to believe that the French people had suddenly become pro-German. Conversely, many others, conscious of the profound and growing resistance of the French, were inclined to consider collaboration either as the acceptance of a *fait accompli* by a few spineless men, or as the policy of a gang of renegades. Collaboration is indeed the slogan of downright traitors, or, at best, the attitude of men of weak purpose. Yet the problem would not be completely solved by the bullets of a firing squad. There are traitors and sycophants, but the lure of 'collaboration with Germany' does not begin or end with them.

The basis for the collaborationist thesis is clear enough and bears some resemblance to elementary logic. It even deceived a few sincere men, though eventually it did not mislead what Michelet describes as 'the intuitive wisdom of the people'. Stated briefly, the case for collaboration is this:

For centuries France has fought to prevent German unity. In most cases—until 1914—she had to fight alone, often against coalitions of Powers which interpreted her struggle with Germany as a French bid for supremacy in Europe. In this struggle, France, although successful for a long time, finally turned out to be the chief sufferer. Yet she could not in the end prevent German unity, with all its implications, because she was too long opposed, and later because she lacked sufficient support. To-day even those nations who fight against Germany are merely aiming at the present German régime but will not threaten German unity. Therefore Germany, although defeated in the field, will in any case have achieved her historical purpose. The German problem will survive in its entirety. In a period of years, France will have to take up arms again and pay the same appalling tribute of blood because she has common frontiers with Germany and because she will never be supported in her contention that the only means of exorcizing the German menace is preventive action dividing and limiting the power of Germany. France will have to perform her recurrent task with gradually diminishing forces. The task is now above her strength. The endless struggle must come to an end. It may be that for years to come, France's national status will be lower than in the past. But a Franco-German combination into which the Germans will infuse new blood, as they did in the days of the early invasions, and to which the French will bring the civilizing and inventive contribution, might appeal to certain minds as a practicable long-term policy. It amounts, in fact, to a revival of Charlemagne's 'Empire of the West', which would become the foundation of a new Europe, unassailable, or at least unconquerable. Peace would be established on lasting foundations.

To this thesis, such arguments as the Bolshevist theory, or the alleged selfishness of Great Britain, are merely incidental. But it will be seen that the collaborationist plea has some semblance of historical and rational backing. The inborn hostility of the French to Germany is described by the advocates of collaboration as the survival of a barbaric instinct unworthy of a civilized nation. And the policy of resistance to Germany is presented as a hopeless perpetuation in modern times of the diplomacy of balance of power of which the only beneficiary—thus the argument runs—has so far been the British Empire.

It is clear that, in practice, the collaborationist thesis is but a specious adaptation to modern times of the famous *Graecia victorem suum vicit*. It affords poor consolation, for this poetical version of events cannot disguise the fact that the sublime and never equalled civilization of Greece became extinct in the process, and that in more than two thousand years nothing has taken the place of the 'Greek miracle'. An alliance with a nation whose deepest motive is precisely the extermination of the very culture which the French offer as their part

of the bargain is an absurdity. Germany is not interested in
French civilization, which, in any case, she despises. But she
is clearly interested in the grabbing of a land which she has
coveted for two thousand years. Nor would the possession
of that land set a limit to her migratory instincts, which feed
on success and receive a stimulus from each new advance in
her centrifugal evolution. The only reason why the Germans
were tempted at all by a *rapprochement* with France was that
it temporarily served their strategy: they wanted to secure the
French fleet and smooth control of all French resources.

In this the French people have been wiser than the theorists.
Their peasant heritage has taught them to judge with deadly
accuracy men's motives and intentions. Behind comprehensive and attractive schemes they perceive the sordid human
calculation. In any case it did not take great perspicacity to
discern it in this particular instance.

From the outset, therefore, there was no desire on the part
of the French people to discuss collaboration as a practical
problem, and less belief that it could be a workable plan. The
theorists were wasting their time in all respects but one. There
is at least one argument put forward by the collaborators which
moves a very sensitive French fibre: that which relates to the
efforts demanded of the French people in time of war and
to the inadequate support which France received against
Germany both in peace and war. This argument found an
echo in French minds long before the armistice raised the
question of collaboration in an acute form, because it corres-
ponds to a profound sense of realism and justice. The French
people may be told that their allies are taking a prominent part
in the war in various fields of action. They accept the statement at its face value. It may be remembered that when,
during the 'phoney war', German loud-speakers were cease-
lessly bellowing at the French soldiers the famous slogan:
'Yes, but where are the British?' the French replied eventually
by raising huge posters above the lines with those words:
'At Narvik.' They were only too eager to emphasize their
allies' active participation in the war. But when the French
army bore the full brunt of the German onslaught, the French
ceased to think in terms of sea ventures and far-flung expeditions. They felt that every other war issue was dwarfed by this
overriding fact: the hurling of German hordes in countless
numbers against the wall of the west. Allied participation then
meant only one thing: troops and more troops. The problem
of equality of sacrifice as well as that of mathematical equilibrium had been raised. And when all was over, the dominant
feeling in France, perhaps more acute than the sense of defeat,

humiliation, and misery, was that of an unprecedented loneliness in Europe.

With this sentiment the Germans have played in more ways than one. In their own mind, even without bitterness, the French people did not conceive that the English could fight on for any length of time, since they had not been able to make more than a limited contribution. And their leaders, through unscrupulousness in some cases, through miscalculation in others, encouraged this conviction. Even those responsible men who admitted that Great Britain might resist invasion, did not believe that she could ever achieve victory single-handed. Either they did not realize that the very resistance of England would have the traditional result of provoking a coalition sooner or later or the anticipation of a Russian participation in this coalition aroused even more distrust than the idea of collaboration with Germany. In this, leaders, apart from the deliberate exploiters of the defeat, were guilty either of blindness, or of weakness, or of misplaced national sense. But the French people as a whole were overwhelmed by an oppressive feeling of solitude. They thought that the old framework of Europe had come to an end. Most of them ceased to believe either that help from outside would come, or that it would come soon enough to be of any avail. That, however, they were ready to acclaim such help if it came, that their hearts had more resilience than their minds, that their faith still lived despite evidence of apparent despair: this was sufficiently illustrated by the tremendous rise of hope and enthusiasm which followed the defeat of the Luftwaffe over Britain in August and September 1940.

Even at the time of the defeat, when France was at the bottom of the pit, there remained a strong body of men in the country who were ready to fight on and a still larger proportion of the French people determined to seize the first occasion of resuming the struggle, and heartened by General de Gaulle's broadcast proclamation from London.

Despite this dynamic element of the population, the Germans might have tricked a greater number of Frenchmen into some form of willing collaboration if they had played a cleverer hand. Their success would not have endured, but they might have achieved some tangible result. However, their old grabbing instincts, those of a people to whom Hitler had restored its predatory instincts and nomadic lawlessness, took precedence over any considerations of long-term policy and future advantage. Germany showed her hand, or rather, her claws, sooner than was good for her.

Hitler had taken a sound line of propaganda in exhibiting

photographs showing his own Guard rendering military
honours to the aged Marshal Pétain. But this was his first
and last concession to the defeated enemy. German chivalry
could go thus far and no farther: it was merely photogenic.

Germany began by imposing an exorbitant tribute: 400
million francs a day. This is over three times the amount of a
heavy French budget in peace time. It is equivalent to a
fourth of the British war budget; and even in times of prosperity the French national revenue is less than a third of the
British. Even so, this fabulous burden was imposed without
prejudice to the financial clauses of the future peace treaty.
The tribute was supposed to cover the expenditure of a German army of occupation totalling four million men. At the
time of writing the German army of occupation had been
reduced to a small fraction of its original strength, but the
war tribute had been reduced by only 25 per cent.

The Germans fixed the rate of the reichsmark without
reference to its purchasing value, at twenty francs to the mark.
At this rate they embarked on a policy of so-called 'purchases'
on a gigantic scale. The sales by the French were naturally
compulsory and amounted to mere requisitions in exchange
for reichsmarks which are completely valueless anywhere, even
in Germany, since she has nothing to sell—except aspirin!

Not only have the Germans shorn the country of both
revenue and capital in money and goods, but they will leave it
mortgaged up to the hilt for a long period of years. Their
own heavy indebtedness had been transmuted by Schacht's
sorcery into French long-term inflation. But the mortgaging
process is not only financial. Whole forests have been felled
and throughout France reafforestation will probably take a
score of years. Agricultural lands have been ruined by forced
changes of production with the intensive use of chemical ferti-
lizers, so that they might yield and yield quickly the exact type
of produce which the Germans required for their own population. Nine-tenths of the French cattle have been slaughtered,
regardless of season and of breeding requirements. Industry,
trade, banks were invaded by hosts of German 'experts' and
gradually *gleichgeschaltet*. This, incidentally, accounts for the
German political hold on some industrialists and bankers,
and for the hesitation of the latter to make a show of frontal
resistance. By plundering France, the Germans were killing
two birds with one stone. In fact, the only difference between
the Germans and the original Huns is that Attila, having no
Dr. Schacht at his disposal, could only pillage what he found
on his path, while Hitler has vastly improved his methods,
inventing a process of pillaging future wealth by methods of

delayed action. They have made sure that a German defeat should mean the economic bankruptcy of France to the same extent as a German victory.

The scope of German looting was apparent in the very first days of the occupation. The French people as a whole were not clearly conscious of its future effects upon French economy. But they were naturally aware of its immediate implications. So long as they could see no hope of rescue, their attitude to the Germans was one of resigned hatred, with occasional and individual outbursts of anger. When it appeared that Hitler had not fulfilled his bombastic promises and was still in Berlin, instead of parading in London, there was a first awakening of hope. That hope became tangible and rose to confidence after the air-battle of Britain. Not only might Germany be defeated, but there was a prospect of France resuming the fight at a later stage. Resistance began to take shape. And problems were set to the individual Frenchman, as they always are when passivity ends and resolution takes its place.

The first problem was Vichy. In the confusion of defeat, the French had looked upon the governments of Bordeaux and Vichy as uninteresting, and possibly inevitable, liquidators of the war. Whether the members of those governments were popular or not mattered little. They were the inescapable accompaniments of defeat. The Marshal had the ungrateful task of negotiating with the conqueror. The majority of the French people sympathized with him in this painful duty, vaguely hoped that his age and reputation might extenuate the rigours of the armistice, and thought that he would lend some dignity to a humiliating negotiation.

The German failure over England threw a different light on the situation. If it were true that the war had not ended with the fall of France, the submission of the French leaders had been perhaps too hasty, so hasty in fact that a growing number of Frenchmen began to question their motives. This suspicion did not extend to the Marshal's motives. But his entourage was not to be trusted. There was at least one man whose past record was shady enough to warrant investigation: Pierre Laval. There might be others. In every Frenchman's mind there began a revision of the 'case for the capitulation' of France. It soon led to the building of a case against the capitulation and the men who had accepted it without exploring every possible alternative.

News broadcasts from England and America had already been listened to before the Battle of Britain. Listening-in became not only a national habit but almost a national duty. Moreover, French soldiers were still fighting by the side of an ally who, far from giving up the struggle, was determined to hit back. If such were the case, American help, which had come too late for France to take advantage of, would now be available to England on a huge scale. There was not only a case against the capitulation, but serious cause for confidence.

Resistance to the Germans became the national watchword, but it had to remain qualified. For the Germans had in their hands the most powerful weapon that a conqueror had ever used against a defeated enemy: one and a half million prisoners of war. This was by far the gravest problem set to every Frenchman. It raised individual, human, and national issues. Nationally it presented the French with a tragic dilemma: either the Germans would return those prisoners in return for exorbitant concessions, by granting which the French would help them in their war effort, or France would reject all demands and a quarter of her adult man-power would be withdrawn from the country for years, and perhaps for ever. Apart from direct human and personal considerations which acted as a deterrent to open resistance, the French demographic problem reappeared in its worst form. Resistance to-day meant a further weakening of France to-morrow, and a catastrophic drop in the birth-rate. This, indeed, was the strongest lever which the Germans could use. It could hardly be hoped that the Germans would respect the laws of war and common humanity. For it was precisely on the assumption of German lawlessness that the French mind rejected the policy of resignation.

The French therefore could only adopt for the time being those methods of resistance which would impair the German effort, increase the German burden, and reduce the effects of any concessions granted to Germany either by the Vichy government or by pro-German elements in French industry and trade.

The notion of 'collaboration' as a policy emerged from the now-famous interview between Marshal Pétain and Hitler in October 1940 at Montoire. In the Marshal's mind, the implications of the word were probably vague and elastic. It might simply mean the recognition of a *fait accompli* and the faithful execution by both parties of the armistice terms. Whether it would involve more than that would depend upon the attitude of Germany and the evolution of the conflict. In Hitler's intentions the object of collaboration was quite clear. It meant using the French as an ally, once Germany had made quite certain that she had gathered into her hands all the means of plundering the country in the present and in the future.

Once more the Germans went too far. They wanted to eat

their cake and have it Their first demonstration of 'collaboration' and of respect for the armistice was the grabbing of
Alsace-Lorraine as an advance on the benefits of the future
peace treaty. This was followed by attempts to set up an
autonomous administration in French Brittany, to arouse disaffection in Flanders, and even in South Lorraine and Burgundy. These efforts ended in complete fiasco. At the same
time, German interference in French industry, trade, banking,
and administration, was growing. In exchange for all this, she
held out vague hopes of releasing a few thousand prisoners.
Perhaps, as a special treat, the French government might be
allowed to return to Paris.

Despite the prospect of a release of prisoners, which, at the
beginning, was taken seriously, 'collaboration' was bitterly
unpopular as soon as the very word was uttered. The majority
of the French people took it as their target for attack, as the
symbol of collusion with the invader and of frustration of their
hopes. Marshal Pétain, whose attitude had been condoned
when it was interpreted as a form of resignation, did not escape
criticism when resignation turned into active co-operation.

For some time Laval's dismissal, which followed closely on
the Montoire interview, appeared to justify the belief that
the Marshal was playing for time. It raised new hopes. But
these were gradually disappointed and, for many Frenchmen,
completely shattered when Darlan took office in February
1941 and began to show his hand. Until that time, a number
of French people still expected Marshal Pétain to voice the
determination of the nation to resist and to use the last levers
which remained in his hands, the Fleet and the Empire, to
counter German exploitation of the French prisoners.

From February 1941 onwards French resistance became
independent of any French authority and was often directed
against certain of the Vichy leaders. Whether Vichy would
produce, in the long run, men capable of more resolution and
energy than the then members of the Government, and
whether Marshal Pétain himself could have shown more
stamina, were matters of speculation. Meanwhile, resistance
would go on.

This dissociation stimulated the people's feelings, but it
created a new and momentous national problem. The division
between the two zones, occupied and unoccupied, which had
originally been purely geographical, began to manifest itself
in political and social affairs.

In the 'free' zone, there was little popular contact with the
Germans. Even when their influence was felt in the form of
requisitions or in the brutal adoption of their police methods,

it led to resentment against the authorities and therefore introduced into the Franco-German feud an element of confusion.
Significantly, the anti-German feeling was, from the outset,
strongest wherever the Germans appeared in person, for instance, in Marseilles harbour, where the population could see
with its own eyes blatant instances of German plundering.

It is perhaps not sufficiently realized that there existed in
Vichy France a social and political ideology independent of
German influences. The so-called National Revolution, which,
incidentally, only bore the German stamp in its police methods
and anti-Jewish legislation, turned out to be a complete
failure. A revolution demands a national surge incompatible
with mental resignation to any form of servitude.

But such notions as economic regionalism and administrative decentralization, restoration of the family as an economic
cell, half-way between the State and the individual, guild
organization as against class organization, and the like, all these
marked, if anything, a return towards a medieval conception
of the State. They corresponded to the latent reaction of a
number of French minds against various shortcomings in the
social system of the Third Republic. The Third Republic,
being what is known as socially progressive, was inclined to lay
stress on the gregarious elements of the nation: industry and
big cities. The advocates of regionalism (the 'blacks') in the
favourable atmosphere of Vichy, took the upper hand. The
Vichy press, in the discussion of social and economic problems
was, in this respect, most illuminating. Although some useful
steps might well be taken in the direction of administrative
decentralization, it is quite obvious that one does not solve a
national problem of social balance merely by reversing or
simply countering a process of development. The public on
the whole showed little interest in the matter.

In the occupied zone, anti-German feeling always ran higher
and expressed itself more forcibly. The difference in 'political
climate' did not, however, express itself only in terms of
popular reaction to the invader. The outlook on social issues
was strikingly different. It was generally 'left-minded', as the
occupied zone comprised the main industrial regions of France
and the ports.

The Germans naturally encouraged this difference of mood
and attitude so as to exploit it to the full. Their propaganda
was fiercely revolutionary in the occupied zone, but in the
south it subtly supported a more conservative policy while
attacking it from the north through the Paris radio. This
division was certainly detrimental to French unity. Moreover,
in North Africa and other overseas territories, a large French

population, which cements the imperial edifice, also remained
with no real contact with occupied France, and little more
with the 'free' zone, save through the *missi dominici* of Vichy,
who were themselves semi-isolated among the French people.

Free French inspiration from London and elsewhere was a
factor of cohesion. Its main effect was to reinforce by en-
couragement and example the dynamic element of the population. But even after resistance was better organized and
active centres increased, it was sometimes difficult to supply
the missing links between various sections of the French
people whose sole common denominator at that moment was
their general hostility to Germany. These groups were not
divided by political controversies, but by the lack of national
exchanges of thought and by the interruption of cultural
currents.

In this respect there was in the French situation at least one
redeeming feature. The occupied zone, which was the most
dynamic part of a divided Empire, was also the most populous
and potentially the strongest, comprising twenty-eight million
inhabitants. It included France's sturdiest provinces (Brittany,
the Northern and Eastern territories, Paris and the Ile de
France) and the largest industrial centres (with the exception
of Saint-Etienne and Le Creusot). This last point was important because collective action might become more valuable in
the future than individual resistance.

It was indeed in the occupied zone that the most striking
anti-German demonstrations took place: the seaports of
Brittany, the industrial centres of Paris, the North, Alsace-
Lorraine, although these centres happened to be the main
targets of the R.A.F. in France. These demonstrations took
every form. In the coastal regions, the graves of fallen British
airmen were daily covered with flowers. Air attacks on the
harbours usually drew large groups of people who expressed
their feelings by acclaiming the raiders and often followed this
up by taking direct action against the German police or
German soldiers. Sabotage was general, despite the ruthless
collective penalties enforced by the Germans. In every factory 'slowing down' was a rule religiously observed. It is estimated that in 90 per cent. of the factories in the occupied
zone the Germans never succeeded in securing more than
half of the expected output. Hardly a day passed without some
attempt on German lives. Demonstrations were also repeatedly organized in unoccupied France, though for obvious
reasons they were seldom acknowledged in official propaganda.
It was, incidentally, a mass meeting at Marseilles, when Yugoslavia rejected her puppet Government, that provoked the

first really stern police measures by Darlan, who took the
Gestapo as a pattern, while at Saint-Nazaire, where the French
had nearly 1,000 casualties, they showed how they would react
to the first sign of an Allied offensive against Germany.

Resistance varied in its methods according to the fortunes
of the war. Any success which brought nearer the prospect
of an Allied invasion of the Continent encouraged boldness.
The French are realists. The clear intention of the people of
France was to help in an Allied victory. But they knew that
open intervention on their part must be properly timed and
coincide with the demands of Allied strategy. Rebellions out
of time would only serve the Germans by exposing to them
the main promoters of a future insurrection against the invader.
It was quite clear to them that if an armed power was not yet in a
position to take a military initiative, a disarmed people was far
less capable of any useful action. German divisions could not
be driven out of France with scythes and pitchforks. Moreover, the fate of the French war prisoners hung in the balance.
The French knew the Germans well. They realized that the
danger of reprisals against their prisoners would recede as the
Germans sensed the approach of defeat, and that with his back
to the wall, the ruthless enemy of to-day would display again
to-morrow his traditional reactions of fear and subservience.
They remembered the time when Germany itself was under
French occupation: far from baiting and challenging the invader as the French themselves were doing now, the Germans
showed humility and obsequiousness. The French are insolent,
sarcastic, and unruly (this last disposition turning under German occupation into an asset). When they made personal
contacts with the Germans, it was generally in order to pile up
demoralizing arguments as to the outcome of the war.

After the failure of the German winter campaign in Russia
and the entry of the United States into the war, confidence in
an Allied victory became virtually unanimous, and temporary
setbacks, recognized as such, had little influence on French
morale. The overwhelming majority of them were now thinking in terms of 'when' and not of 'if'. In 1942 the only
apparent results of Allied reverses were signs of impatience,
not of despondency. The process of mental rearmament was
by now complete.

The very resistance of the French people to the intruder
raised problems beyond that of a resumption of the struggle,
for which they were certainly ready. Hatred of the invader and
yearning for freedom were the primary causes of that resistance. But it derived stimulus and impulse from a variety of
sources. So individual views on a post-war France varied. In

spite of enemy occupation, which creates a common purpose, a nation does not remain static. Resistance may have been stimulated by social as well as national considerations. The success of Russia in checking the German armies, for instance, emboldened the most politically advanced section of the population, whose activity had hitherto been sporadic. On the other hand the growing Russian contribution to an Allied victory proved a source of anxiety for the more conservative elements, although the French on the whole laid stress on the military rather than the ideological aspect of the Russian problem. The American entry into the war aroused hopes not only among the majority of Frenchmen whose primary aim was the defeat of Germany at all costs, but even in quarters which did not previously believe in a British victory and were apprehensive of a Russian one.

While the foremost French preoccupation, the defeat of the German invader, overrode every other consideration, various incalculable factors came into play. Though rejected on national grounds, German propaganda might yet find echoes in the social field. When Radio Paris pointed out instances of social injustice, they might well be noted and remembered by the working class for future reference, although they did not provoke immediate reactions. The complacency of some industrial and financial magnates towards Germany might also affect the French social outlook at a later date, and, by a strange paradox, capitalist collaboration, where it existed, and revolutionary propaganda against capitalism by the Germans, might thus accumulate and result in encouraging a leftward trend.

On the other hand the peasantry, which sometimes proved more successful than the urban population in cheating the German plunderers, might have learned by such accidental experience to appreciate the advantages of a relative economic independence. This would seem to encourage a process of regionalism which the propaganda of Vichy and Lyons had tried to initiate in the 'free' zone. Finally, the political and social trend of thought in Great Britain, America, and Russia, respectively, was bound to have some influence on a nation which looked to external intervention on the Continent for its liberation.

All these elements of the French situation must be borne in mind and one statement at least may be made with some emphasis: The interests of French internal unity and balance coincide with those of European equilibrium on one capital point—the need for the largest possible Anglo-Saxon contribution to the relief of the Continent in the military as well as in the economic and political fields.

A substantial Anglo-Saxon participation in Continental operations was bound not only to ensure a greater measure of European co-operation and by bringing stabilizing factors into play prevent rifts in the social structure from affecting the common purpose; it would in the first place rally in most countries, and particularly in France, forces which had remained relatively inactive. Many French officers, diplomats, civil servants, who have never been collaborators either in fact or in intention, accepted the *status quo* out of pessimism or misplaced loyalty, or miscalculation, or with the remote hope of rendering services at a later date. These men were good patriots. In most cases, they believed that their presence might limit the damage, and expected that France might temporarily have to follow the inglorious line of policy which Stresemann described by the German word *finassieren*.

It must be realized that once the armistice had been signed and French military and naval power paralysed, the attitude of many Frenchmen may genuinely have ceased to be dictated by their own severe judgement of the capitulation and by a purely 'Allied' conception of the war. Many patriots, rightly or wrongly, thought that since France had suffered the odium of the armistice, their main duty was to limit its effects. The problem of a resumption of the fight and of the Alliance might arise later, in which case they would be ready. Meanwhile they had to turn to very grave French problems. That a quarter of the male population of France should be withdrawn, perhaps for ever, from the social and biological life of the nation, that the whole economic system of France should be broken for several generations: those were not matters which could be dismissed as second in importance to a sporadic contribution to the pursuit of the war. And after all, the pressure not only of the French people but of many elements of the civil service, of the diplomatic service, and of the army, must have remained strong, since the Germans in April 1942 had to admit failure and to force Laval back into the Vichy government.

There have therefore been many forms of resistance with different methods, different inspirations, though with a common aim. These differences were not immaterial, despite the similarity of the purpose. They could best be reconciled by a large Anglo-Saxon participation in the military defeat of Germany. In this respect, the importance of the American contribution cannot be over-emphasized. It is a force for unity, an element on which every section of French opinion holds the same views. In the foreign field it certainly is the lowest common denominator.

More generally, it can be said that the French would wish the Anglo-Saxon Powers to have as wide a share as possible in the organization of victory and peace. They feel a great respect for the Russian army, which has confounded all calculations and all assessments of its true strength. The resistance of Russia following the defeat of France has given the French no sense of humiliation. They had noted that Russia, before she could take the initiative in her turn, had to lose for strategic reasons stretches of territory three times as large as the total area of metropolitan France, and that her losses in men, according to the most conservative estimates, must have reached figures which would have been utterly inconceivable in the case of France, whose male population amounts to less than a quarter of Russia's. The average Frenchman has, on the whole, little fear of a Russian ideological *diktat*. At the same time the experience of this war has shown him the possible implications of demographic inferiority. His eyes will be turned to the West for a counterpoise, especially when it is supplied by nations whose way of life has for many generations kept pace with his own on fundamental issues. His only fear is lest the Anglo-Saxon Powers, after they have achieved their primary aim, the destruction of hitlerism and of the German war machine, might once more underestimate the German danger in making the peace settlement. For every Frenchman, there is only one German problem, of which hitlerism is but an aspect. The French have no sentimental hatred for the Germans, except of course in circumstances like the present. They simply consider Germany as a dangerous biological problem. Their attitude to Germany is dictated by the French will to survive as themselves and as part of a civilization which periodically is in peril of being absorbed by German migrations. Until such time as Germany gives evidence of stability and fixity, this will remain the French attitude. And many Frenchmen will think in their hearts that there is little difference between fighting only hitlerism and giving up the fight with Germany altogether.

What French régime will emerge from this great crisis cannot be conjectured. Democratic the French certainly are—in their beliefs, in their life, in their blood. One might say paradoxically that they would live democratically under any régime. They are passionately attached to the freedom of political institutions. But the conception of freedom is not an answer to every problem in the twentieth century, and France has learned it to her cost. Life under German occupation has naturally created a yearning for liberty in all its forms. At the same time the military defeat has taught them a lesson.

VII. IN PARIS

1. CAFÉ ON A BOULEVARD
(Margot Lubinski)

2. BOOK AND PRINT STALLS ON THE QUAYS
(Margot Lubinski)

Even under the German heel, tendencies began to appear leading towards the idea of an improved social system, a stronger executive, a greater reliance on real values, on practical programmes rather than ideologies, and on men rather than on parties as such. These ideas do not differ substantially from the apparent trend of thought in England. They are coupled with a violent detestation of those régimes which have left across Europe a trail of blood and stupid destruction. The trials of France can only have strengthened in her people a sense of individual responsibility towards the community, which has become an indispensable contribution to the reconciliation of diverse and often conflicting conceptions.

In the French defeat and in France's present plight, the existence of a sturdy peasantry has proved to be a valuable asset. In her recovery this reservoir of physical strength will play a great part. But the problem of French adaptation to economic and social world development will subsist. It may be that she will have to sacrifice some cherished traditions. She will certainly have to rebuild her economic and social framework on new foundations and to redress her balance of population in a way more suitable to her international status. The old French conviction that the birth-rate increased in direct ratio to the numerical strength of the agricultural population, has been strikingly belied by the demographic evolution of England and Germany in the last hundred years. The population of Great Britain increased threefold as a consequence of the Industrial Revolution, while that of France was increasing by only one-third. French agriculture must remain a source of wealth to the French nation and, probably, must be granted some measure of economic and administrative decentralization. Yet this must be reconciled with a process of industrial concentration. It serves no useful purpose to maintain a rural population unable, in the face of world prices, to enjoy those standards of living which alone can redress the curve of the French birth-rate. Moreover, France must remember her international mission in common with other great civilizing nations and her part in the maintenance of world order. Her means must be adequate to that mission, which she neither can nor will abdicate.

In her long history, she has never failed to solve the problems raised by her own destiny, which is inseparable from that of Western civilization. She is to-day confronted by new and momentous issues: her demographic and economic balance. She will face them with an energy and sense of responsibility born of her very trials. They are not beyond her strength, her powers of adaptation, and her resilience. It may be that unanimity in action will not be achieved without a struggle, but whatever the case may be, she will emerge from the storm united and strong.

Another forecast may be ventured: the régime or, rather, the new order which will be set up in post-war France will spring from the people and from the heart of the country. The liberators will be acclaimed, but only the sufferings and travail of a people on its national soil can produce the phoenix-like process of rebirth.

To bring about a resurrection the French earth will supply the men from among those who undertook the perilous and inspiring mission of facing and challenging their German jailers every day; from among those who realized the cost of freedom in the agonized beating of their own hearts; from among those who saw women weep and children die, and who still kept faith.

CHAPTER XI

ENGLAND AND FRANCE

FOR many Englishmen the French problem has been a subject of irritation during the last few years. It was natural enough that for many of them the fate of France should be a matter of indifference. On the vast war-map embracing every continent, France is but a spot. Apart from the strategic issue involved in the future of the French fleet, there was a tendency to think of France as a second-rate factor in the development of Europe, and to regard her with bitterness, indulgence, or nostalgia, according to mood and knowledge. The feelings of a people at war are governed by the exigencies of war, its judgements by expediency: that is inevitable. The man who goes out to fight has little time for objective judgement or for historic study. Three general notions which are clear and convenient therefore guided the average Englishman in his outlook on the French question: France broke her undertaking when she signed the armistice; leading Frenchmen collaborated with Germany; the French people prevented neither the armistice nor the collaboration. These notions are qualified by the knowledge that free Frenchmen continued the fight, and by the occasional (and not general) belief that there was among the French people resistance to active collaboration. Unfortunately, these qualifications do not substantially alter the picture. The value of any French alliance is therefore questioned on several grounds:

doubtful military strength in the future, doubtful reliability, doubtful goodwill on the part of the French themselves. This picture, set against that of the might of Russia and America, suffers in many English minds from the comparison.

The sequence of events, the light in which France has shown herself, the circumstances in which English judgements were formed, explain this severe assessment of the French question and of its relative importance in the world. It may be said that, apart from faults in leadership, the defeat of France and her subsequent attitude can be traced to causes and motives not in themselves blameworthy, but this is the French side of the affair. What matters more to English people than the intrinsic merits of the French case, is the answer to the question: What will be the value to England of the friendship of a restored France? Although there may be a widespread feeling in Britain that this value is not very considerable, I contend that it is as great to Britain as that of British friendship may be to France.

But first to sum up the causes of the defeat: France was defeated in the first place because she was directly exposed to the German impact, which, at the time, no single nation could have resisted alone; in the second place because her manpower and economic system, as they emerged from the last war and from twenty years of latent revolution, were not sufficient to bear the impact of a hyper-industrialized and highly populated nation; in the third place because this man-power and economic potential had not been marshalled to the full, chiefly because of social and political instability; in the fourth place because her High Command was not adequate, and her civil administration had been weakened by the French crisis. These were the determining factors of the defeat. They were grave, but inherent in a process of transformation which all nations have to undergo, and which cannot be suddenly resolved even by a national reaction to external danger. Other factors—such as the behaviour of politicians, the Fifth Column, individual acts of treason or cowardice—were of secondary importance and in different circumstances would have been immaterial or irrelevant.

But even had France at the time of the German onslaught been in a state of complete, adequate, up-to-date preparation, it is still doubtful whether she alone could have done more than hold the German drive until substantial help from outside, direct and vast military help, had re-established the balance between a nation of thirty-nine millions (without its dependencies) and a nation of nearly eighty millions.

The emphasis in most English minds is laid on French

VIII. FRANCE WILL RISE AGAIN

deficiencies. All Frenchmen are agreed in recognizing that the primary responsibility for their defence was their own and that they did not sufficiently discharge it; but most of them are equally agreed, without the slightest bitterness, that a successful fight against Germany could not have been carried out on the basis of a limited Allied contribution—that is, on a contribution not exceeding that which had been agreed to by the French High Command in 1939: a maximum of thirty divisions towards the end of 1940. Most Frenchmen know by now that the British executed their undertakings and that at the time of the May offensive the divisions promised by that date had been sent. They merely record the fact that those undertakings were inadequate to the task and would have proved such in almost any circumstances, barring the hypothesis of incompetence and inadequacy in German war preparations (a defect with which that warlike people can, alas, seldom be charged). This point of view based on the hard realities of figures must be borne in mind, since it accounts for the fact that, in giving up the fight, most Frenchmen did not feel as guilty of a breach of contract as they would in different circumstances. It also accounts for their lack of confidence, at the time of the armistice, in the British capacity to stem the German tide. Finally, the feeling that, although in disorder and ultimately in chaos, they nevertheless prolonged the retreat after all hope of resisting on metropolitan soil had been abandoned, and that the French army thereby allowed the British a short but invaluable respite, also contributed towards blunting their sense of contractual failure. This sense was later stimulated by the moral courage of England and the generous speech made by her Prime Minister.

After two years during which they kept even with the Germans, the French thought only in terms of their contribution to victory, a contribution made by those Frenchmen who fought underground and those who, in the most difficult circumstances and through the hardest trials, succeeded in reaching Britain in numbers limited by their means only and not by their goodwill.

But the French problem, from a British point of view, far exceeds in scope that of a contribution to ultimate victory, the tangible proof of a will to liberation and freedom from the German yoke which could not be doubted—although it may have been clouded—for it is written in two thousand years of French history. To assess the importance of France in the future of the British Empire, some facts must be faced squarely and borne in mind.

The present war, though we cannot yet measure its full

effects, has brought some realities into relief. It has shown how and with what consequences German unity could be accomplished. Whether or not Austria, the Sudetens, and other German-speaking communities were willing to join the Reich, the fact remains that a powerful nationalist movement could rally them and make them fight Europe under German banners; and that German unity meant a bid for world conquest. There are in Europe some eighty million Germans and the least that can be said is that their self-dedication to peaceful pursuits in the future cannot be taken for granted. The war has also shown the considerable military potentialities of Russia, a nation of 180 millions, which are not likely to diminish in the future. It has also proved that Italy, which counted among the foremost European states, cannot attain the status of a great military nation even after twenty years of clamorous militarism, since six French divisions indifferently equipped held thirty Italian divisions in June 1940, and a handful of British troops conquered the vast army of Graziani. The main reservoirs of strength, man-power, and resources on the Continent (leaving France apart for the moment) are therefore Germany and Russia.

Great Britain is at present at war with the one and associated with the other. But a nation must think in terms not only of her present situation but of her permanent existence in a changing world. Britain, a country of forty-five million inhabitants, is situated at the extreme edge of a continent whose development cannot be foreseen but whose main demographic features are two ethnical communities of outstanding size. It may be that some European organization, perhaps federal, can be set up whereby relative security will be ensured. Security must however remain hypothetical so long as Europe has not completed her social and international evolution, for deliberate will-to-war by a nation or several nations is not the sole cause of conflict, and it would be madness to suppose that after this war Europe will reach her final stage by a mere process of political planning, however far-sighted be the settlement.

For long, Great Britain was the sole trustee of Western civilization in the true sense. All the other countries of Europe which are the heirs to this civilization were under direct or indirect German control. The misery and turmoil left behind by the now receding German tide is such that, physically and morally, European civilization has suffered a severe setback.

Should France be forced, through a final breakdown of her ties with England, into gradual subordination to any of the stronger ethnical groups in Europe, the position of Great Britain would become, in the long run, far more serious than

at the time when Joseph Chamberlain realized the need for a
Continental alliance. The facile answer to this argument is, of
course, that such a conception of Europe smacks of 'balance of
power'. But, in one form or another, either because one thinks
in terms of 'nations' or because one has to reckon with powerful demographic elements, it is impossible to avoid the notion
of balance of power so long as complete uniformity in national
and social habits has not been achieved. The thing is a reality:
the word must therefore be accepted. The mere desire to preserve our civilization, both Christian and socially progressive,
as against other conceptions of common life, demands that we
should think in terms of a balance of power. Any coalition in
war, any system of collective security in peace, is only, after all,
an improved application of that well-understood policy of
balance of power.

The parting of the ways between England and France would
have an inevitable consequence; the law of gravitation would
eventually draw France into the orbit of the vaster ethnical
groups and leave England permanently in the very position in
which she found herself as a result of war exigencies, that of
an outsider. But she was an outsider to whom every nation
looked with hope and confidence. In years to come, should
France and England give up common ideals and common
policies, Europe would in fact, despite any theoretical recon-
structions, be shaped or shape itself according to a process
of development in which the Western factor would play a
smaller and smaller part, in which the Western civilization
would be merged into Central or Eastern demographic groups.
In accepting this, we should be making on a tremendous scale
the same mistake as those Frenchmen who believed that French
civilization could survive its merger with the Germanic
folk.

We must be under no delusion: under Nazi rule or otherwise, in victory or in defeat, the Germanic stream follows its
natural course: which is towards the absorption of Western
elements. We think in terms of a way of life, of political and
ethical culture, of communities cemented by a moral, spiritual,
and intellectual tradition. German demographic expansion
goes on, and grows by leaps and bounds when the German
components are gathered together. Moreover, German unity,
though shattered by war, can be re-achieved by propaganda
in London or in New York as well as by political means
in Berlin. The great fear of every good German to-day,
whether a National-Socialist or not, whether fighting in Hitler's legions or an exile, is not that his country may suffer
from the war, that its progress may suffer a setback, but that

German unity may be threatened by the victorious powers. And there is, to this fear, a complementary one, its political corollary, that the Western Powers, great and small, may be at last closely and finally united in the far-sighted and generous way suggested by Mr. Winston Churchill when he offered the French government the chance to form with England a federal unit. The work of dissociation between England and France, the greatest German aim after German unity, goes on even outside German-shackled Europe. It goes on in articles, books, and pamphlets, whether these pronounce the final condemnation of France or proclaim its decay; it goes on, as a corollary to those articles, books, and pamphlets, in every man born among the German folk who asserts the possibility of a united and yet pacific Germany.

For centuries, in peace and war, sometimes with ruthless tenacity (as in Richelieu's time), sometimes in desperate self-defence (as in the last war), France has stood a barrier to German expansion towards the West, as a Western dyke to a flood which might at any moment submerge our civilization. She has occasionally absorbed some of those active Germanic elements, which, in controllable doses, bring a strong and welcome influx of new blood, but which, fully released, would have fatal consequences for the Western world. It is not suggested that French policy has always resorted to irreproachable methods, nor that it has not often gone beyond its task, as under Louis XIV and especially Napoleon. Yet whatever progress has been achieved in Europe within the framework of Western laws and culture is largely due to this guardianship, towards which England made, by different methods and even through her quarrels and conflicts with France, an equally vast contribution. This common task the two nations have performed not only in Europe, but throughout the five continents, together with the Spaniards, Dutch, Italians, Portuguese: it has been performed despite faults, abuse of power, injustice, war, which are the inevitable failings of men. It has been achieved by countries which are, morally and spiritually, the heirs to the Roman and Christian Empire, whether the legacy was transmitted directly or otherwise. Though the world has witnessed great German achievements by individuals, it still awaits the constructive aspects of German civilization in the realm of common life. We can hope for them; but we cannot in that hope afford to renounce or impair our heritage. This heritage is still retained primarily by England and France.

We do not know whither this war is leading us. We know very well what we are fighting for. We are fighting to keep this heritage, not as a dead weight, as an immutable system, but as a basis, as a foundation for any edifice which we may erect, and as a dam to regulate inevitable social changes and transformations. In that struggle, France has gone down under the armed might of the German hordes. But she must not and will not be counted out. The whole life of France under Germany became a constant and murmuring plebiscite of the whole nation: a plebiscite against German rule, a plebiscite for freedom, a plebiscite for a resumption of the struggle, for the pursuit of France's mission in Europe. Yet she could not resume it alone. Neither the fact that she was struck in the midst of a process of development which had temporarily weakened her, nor the faults of military leaders and politicians, can hide the inadequacy of a single nation to hold the wall of the West, even if she knows that the great might of England will gradually back her endeavour with equal force. Now the legions of England and America march through the Continent and the French nation rises and marches with them. Later a still greater task will confront liberators and liberated. From West and East, from America and Russia, contributions to victory far greater than the rise of the French people have come to support a once lonely England. Yet, when those great armies have returned to their peaceful pursuits, there will still lie, across twenty miles of sea, the land of France. It will be raised again by the hands of men of French stock, as it has been raised before from even greater depths to high individual and national achievements. But it rests largely with England to decide whether this force, which will ever survive, shall in the future gravitate around a centralized Europe, or preserve with England and other nations the independence of Western culture and its unique contribution to the progress of a free Europe.

INDEX

Academicians, 82, 96, 97
Agrarians, 42
Agriculture, 5, 75, 76, 77
Aldington, Richard, 93 n.
Algeria, 11, 14, 34
Aliens in France, 89 and n.
Alsace-Lorraine, 11, 20, 29, 35, 68, 118,
    120
America. See United States
Amsterdam Conference (1905), 88
Anti-Jewish legislation, 119
Antwerp, 30
Apollinaire, Guillaume, 62, 98
Arlan, Marcel:
    L'Ordre, 98
Architecture, 53
Armée de l'Est, 110
Armistice (1918), 38, 68, 72
— (1940), 111, 127
Art, 60, 63, 94
Assemblée Constituante, 28, 29
Augsburg, League of, 22
Austria, 23, 29, 30, 32, 33, 34, 35, 72, 131
Autarky, 77, 78 and n., 81, 84
Avignon, 53–4

Bainville, Jacques, 31
Balance of power, 21, 72, 132
Balzac, 42, 60, 61
    Lys dans la Vallée, 51
    Comédie Humaine, 61
Barrès, Maurice, 63
Barthou, Louis, 68, 71
Bastille, 24
Baudelaire:
    Fleurs du Mal, 61–2
Beaumarchais, 57
Belgium, 30, 32, 33, 105, 106, 107, 108
Bell, Clive, 53
Benda, Julien:
    La trahison des Clercs, 93 and n., 98
Berl, Emanuel, 97
Berlin, 5, 132
Berlioz, 61
Bernadnos, Georges, 96
    Les Grands Cimetières sous la Lune, 102
Berthelot, Marcellin, 39
Bir Hacheim, 111
Birth-rate, 11, 67, 92, 117, 126. See also
    Demographic problem; Population
Bismarck, 35
'Blacks', 42, 43, 44, 89, 91, 119
'Blasés', 44
'Blues', 39
Blum, Léon, 87
Bourbons, 26, 33
Bourgeoisie, 24, 34, 42, 97
Bourget, Paul, 94
Britain, Battle of, 114, 116
Brittany, 43, 118, 120
British Empire, 130
Brunswick, Duke of, 30
Burckhardt, 67
Burgundy, 118
Byzantium, 7

Calas, Jean, 57
Calvinism, 55
Cambon, Jules and Paul, 21, 39
Canada, 80
Cartel des Gauches, 88
Casualties, war, 68
Céline, Louis-Ferdinand, 98

Centralization, 46
Cézanne, 63
Chamberlain, Joseph, 132
Chamfort, Nicolas, 57
Chanson de Roland, 53
Chaplin, Charlie, 99
Chardin, 58
Charlemagne, 21, 52, 62, 112
Charles V of Habsburg, 21
Charles X, 33
Chateaubriand:
    Athala, 60,
    Les Mémoires d'Outre-Tombe, 60
Chronique de l'Œil de Bœuf, 8
Church. See Roman Catholic Church
Churchill, Winston, 130, 133
Cinema, the, 99
Civil Service, 39
Citröen, 82
Class war, 86, 88, 91
Classical Age, 24, 52, 55, 56, 57
Claudel, Paul, 96
Clootz, Anacharsis, 43
Colette, 94, 97
Collaboration, Franco-German, 111 ff.
    127
Collapse of France. See Defeat of F.
Collectivist dogmas, 33
Colonial Empire, French. See Empire
Colourist painters, 60
Commune, Paris (1789–91), 28; (1871), 33,
    36
Communists, 39, 45, 88, 89, 90, 91, 97
Comte, Auguste, 61
Condillac, Etienne:
    Traité des Sensations, 58
Congress of Paris (1856), 35
— of Vienna (1815), 33
Conscientious objection, 45
Conscription, 44–5
Conservatives, 42
Constitution. See English C.; French C.
Convention Nationale, 30, 31
Corneille, 55
Corot, 48, 63
Corporativism, 90
Corruption, 100
Couperin, 58
Courbet, 63
Craftsmanship, 56
Crimean War (1854–6), 35
Czechoslovakia, 74

Daladier, Edouard, 90
Dams, 82
D'Annunzio, 7
Darlan, Admiral, 118, 121
Daudet, Alphonse, 63
— Léon, 63
Debussy, 63
Decentralization, 119
Déclaration des Droits de l'Homme, 25,
    29
Degas, Hilaire-Germain, 63
Degas the elder, 44
De Gaulle, General Charles, 114
Defeat of France (1940), 7, 8, 103 ff., 134
Defeatism, 104
Delacroix, 60
Democracy, 40
Demographic problem, 66 ff., 75, 92, 103,
    117, 124, 126, 132
Derain, André, 41

Descartes, 55
Determinism, 50
Devonshire, Duke of, 40
Dictatorship of the Proletariat, 39
Directory (1795), the, 25, 31
Dowries, 41, 42
Dreyfus Case, 93
Dualism, 42, 46, 92
Dufretay, M., 81
Duhamel, Georges, 82, 94
   Civilisation, 97
   Salavins, 97
Dunkirk, 109

Eguzon dam, 82
Egypt, 32
Electrification, 82–3
Elite, the, 97, 100, 102
Empire, French Colonial, 11, 12, 13, 14,
   27, 36, 67, 118, 119, 120
Encyclopedists, 52, 56, 57, 59, 89
Endemic Revolution, 83 ff., 97, 103
Engels, Friedrich, 33
England. *See* Great Britain
English Constitution, 25
Ersatz, 78
Etats-Généraux, 26, 28
Expansionism, German, 20, 22, 32–3, 36
   65, 70, 132

Family life, 41, 42, 45, 46, 119
Fifth Column, 29, 128
First Empire, 36
— Republic, 30
Fiscal policy, 27, 28
Flanders, 15, 30, 32, 118
Foch, Marshal Ferdinand, 38
Foreigners in France. *See* Aliens
Fourier, François, 33
France, Anatole, 63
Francis I, 54
Franco-Prussian War (1870-1), 13, 62
Franco-Russian Pact, 71
Frederick the Great, 35
Frederick II, 23, 29, 32, 57
Frederick William II, 29
Free French, 12, 120
French Academy, 82, 96, 97
— Constitution, 26, 36
— Empire, First, 36
— —, Second, 35, 36
— —, Colonial. *See* Empire
— Republic, First, 30
— —, Second, 34
— —, Third, 11, 25, 36, 38
— Revolution, 11, 23, 24 ff., 32, 33, 34,
   36, 38, 39, 40, 43, 51, 57, 61, 85, 88

Geneva Protocol, 69
Géricault, Théodore, 60
Germany, *passim*.
Gide, André, 94, 97
Giraudoux, Hippolyte, 41, 97, 98
   Bella, 97
Gobineau, Comte de, 39
Great Britain, 9, 11, 23, 30, 32, 33, 34, 35,
   36, 66-7, 68, 69, 70 and *n.*, 71, 72, 74,
   76, 85, 89, 93, 113, 114, 122, 131–4
Great War. *See* World War I
Greece, 48, 112

Habsburgs, 22, 23, 32, 35
Hannibal, 7
Henri IV, 16, 21
Hitler, Adolf, 20, 39, 67, 71, 72, 78 *n.*,
   92, 93, 103 ff, 114 ff., 132

Hitlerism, 99, 124
Hugo, Victor:
   Les Misérables, 60
   Les Chansons des Rues et des Bois, 60
   Choses Vues, 60
   Hernani, 61
Hundred Years War, 52, 53

Ibsen, Henrik;
   The Master Builder, 48
Ideologies, 85, 89, 90, 91, 93, 101, 119–24
Impressionist painters, 52, 55, 63
Individualism, 41, 42, 46, 99
Industrial classes, 47, 75, 91
Industry and industrial power, 5, 11, 75
   76, 77, 82, 84, 86, 92
Ingres, Jean, 61
Internationalism, 45
Invasions of France, 18, 21, 105 ff.
Iron mines, 77
Italy, 12, 31, 35, 48, 54, 90, 111, 131

Jacobinism, 42
Jemmappes, 30
Jeunesses Agricoles Chrétiennes, 102
Jeunesses Ouvrières Chrétiennes, 102
Jews, 103, 119
Journalism, 99

Kernan, Thomas;
   Report on France, 42, 43
Kropotkin, Prince Peter, 59, 97

Labiche, Eugène, 42
Lancret, Nicolas, 58
Land, the, 45, 46
Language, 52, 62
Laval, Pierre, 71, 115, 116, 123
Law's system of credit, 25
League of Augsburg, 22
— of Nations, 69, 71
Lebensraum, 20
Legislative Assembly, 29
'Liberté, Egalité, Fraternité', 24, 43
Literature, 50 ff., 93
Louis XI, 16, 21, 53, 54
— XII, 54
— XIV, 8, 22, 24, 55, 57, 133
— XV, 58
— XVI, 30
— XVIII, 33
Louis-Napoleon Bonaparte. *See* Napo-
   leon III
Louis-Philippe, 33, 34, 44
Ludendorff, Erich von, 39
Lyautey, Marshal Louis, 13, 14

Maginot Line and policy, 104-5, 107
Malraux, André, 97
Malta, 32
Manet, Edouard, 63
Man-power, 13, 68, 107
Marèges dam, 82
Marie-Antoinette, 28
Marivaux, Pierre, 58
Marx, Karl, 33, 87
Marxism, 87, 88
Mauriac, François, 96, 97
Mauritius, 32
Maurras, Charles, 96
Maximilian, Ferdinand, Emperor of
   Mexico, 35
Mazarin, 31
Mechanized industry, 82
Mehmet Ali, 34

Mérimée, Prosper, 61
  Carosse du Saint-Sacrement, 61
Mexico, 35
Michelet, Jules, 111
Molière, 56, 57
Monarchy and monarchism, 29, 36, 39, 44
Montaigne, 50, 54–5, 57, 58, 60
Montespan, Mme de, 8
Montesquieu, 56, 57, 75
Montherlant, Henri de, 94, 99
Montoire (Pétain-Hitler) interview, 117, 118
Morocco, 11, 13
Munich crisis, 83
Mysticism, 57, 58

Napoleon Bonaparte (Napoleon I), 8, 25, 30 ff., 36, 59, 62, 133
Napoleon III, 34–5
Napoleonic wars, 31 ff.
National-Socialism, 90, 132
Nature, 58, 59, 61
Nazis, 5
Nerval, Gérard de, 60, 61
Nietzscheism, 99
Normandy, 14

Oxford, 5

Painting, 52, 53, 54, 55, 58, 62–3
Paris, 5, 15, 17, 28, 42, 47, 101, 118, 119
Paris Commune. See Commune
— Congress of (1856), 35
— riots in (1934), 90
Parnassus, School of, 62
'Parti Ouvrier et Paysan', 87
Party Conference of Tours (1922), 88
Pascal, Blaise, 50, 56
Peasantry, 5, 39, 41, 42, 44, 47, 76, 78, 86, 87, 91, 93
Péguy, Charles, 63
Peninsula, the, 35
Permanent Revolution, 83 ff., 97, 103
Pétain, Marshal Henri, 97, 115 ff.
'Phoney war' (1939–40), 107, 113
'Pléiade', poets of the, 54, 57
Poincaré, Raymond, 96, 97
Poland, 30, 35, 48, 106, 108
Popular Front, 84, 91
Population problems, 11, 17, 36, 68, 74, 75, 104, 124. See also Demographic problem
Populistes, 51, 98
Positivism, 61
Prices, 92
Prisoners of war (1940), 78, 117
Pritchard incident, 34
Private property, 86, 87
Prix Goncourt, 98
Proletariat, 39, 84, 85, 87. See also Industrial Classes
Protectionism, 80–1
Proust, Marcel, 63
  Le Côté de Guermantes, 56
Prussia, 22, 23, 29, 30, 32, 33, 34, 35
Pupier, Jean;
  France d'hier, France de demain, 43

Rabelais, 54, 55
Racine, 56, 60
Radicals, 29
Radio Paris, 119, 122
Rameau, Jean Philippe, 58
'Reds', 42, 44, 89, 91
Reformation, 54

Regency, the, 58
Regionalism, 39, 119
Religion, 46, 54
Religious wars, 55
Renaissance, 24, 52, 54, 63
Renan, Ernest, 63
Renault, 82
Renoir, Pierre Auguste, 63
Republic. See First R., Second R., Third R.
Revolution, Endemic, 83 ff., 97, 103
— (1789). See French R.
— (1848), 44
— (1871). See Commune
Reynaud, Paul, 8, 14
Rhine, Rhine frontier, and Rhineland 13, 21, 22, 30, 32, 35, 65, 72
Richelieu, 21, 22, 26, 31, 133
Rimbaud, Jean Arthur, 52, 60, 62
Riots in Paris (6 Feb. 1934), 90
Riou, Gaston;
  Europe, ma Patrie, 96
Robespierre, 30
Rodin, Auguste, 63
Roman Catholic Church, 23, 42, 43, 46, 54, 100 ff.
Romanticism, 42, 50, 52, 59, 60, 61, 62, 94
Rome, 7, 22, 101
Rops, Daniel;
  Notre Inquiétude, 96
Rousseau, 42, 51, 56, 57, 58, 59, 62
  Contrat Social, 59
  Émile, 59
Royalists, 39. See also Monarchy
Ruhr, 69
'Rush to the Frontiers', the, 44
Russia, 11, 30, 33, 35, 36, 66, 67, 71, 74, 91, 103, 107, 114, 121, 124, 128, 131, 134
Russian Revolution (1917), 36, 88

Sabotage, 120
Sadowa, 35
St. Helena, 32
Saint-Exupéry, Antoine de, 96
Saint-Nazaire, 121
Saint-Simon, Comte de, 33, 56, 60
Schacht, Dr. Hjalmar, 103, 115
Second Empire, 35, 36
— International, 88
— Republic, 34
Section Française de l'Internationale Ouvrière (S.F.I.O.), 87 and n.
Sedan, 107
Seven Years War, 23
Shaw, Bernard, 27
Silk-weaving, 76
Simon, Sir John, 70 n.
Socialists, 87, 88–9
Soubise family, 27
Spain, 22, 30, 74
Spanish Civil War, 90, 102
Stavisky scandal, 100
Stendhal [Marie-Henri Beyle], 60, 61
  The Red and the Black, 42
  La Chartreuse de Parme, 61
Stresemann, Gustav, 71, 123
Sturm und Drang, 62, 96
Sudetens, 72, 131
Summer, Dr., 20
Surrealism, 98
Syria, 13, 32

Tailhade, Laurent, 54
Talleyrand, 8, 33

Terror, the, 30
Third International, 88
— Reich, 20, 69, 71, 72, 104, 131
— Republic, 11, 12, 25, 38, 91, 99, 100
Thirty Years War, 23, 32, 36, 68
Totalitarianism, 91
Trade Unionism, 85
Treaty of Locarno (1925), 69
— of Picquigny (1477), 23
— of Versailles (1919), 69, 70, 71, 72
— of Westphalia (1648), 22
Tunis, 111
Turenne, Marshal Vicomte de, 72

U.S.S.R. *See* Russia
United States of America, 70 and *n*., 74,
    82, 85, 99, 107, 121, 128, 133

Valéry, Paul, 97
Valmy, 30
Vendée, 39
Versailles, 28
— Treaty (1919), 69, 70, 71, 72
Vichy Government, 5, 116 ff.
Vienna, Congress of (1815), 33
Villon, François, 53, 60

Voltaire, 18, 29, 44, 56, 57, 58

Wages, 84, 92
War-potential, 78
Wars:
    Crimean War, 34–5
    Franco-Prussian War, 13, 62
    Hundred Years War, 52, 53
    Napoleonic Wars, 31 ff.
    Religious wars, 55
    Seven Years War, 23
    Thirty Years War, 23, 32, 36, 68
    War of the Austrian Succession, 23
    War of the Spanish Succession, 22
    World War I, 11, 13, 52, 63, 67, 68, 70,
        77, 85, 88, 94, 96, 101, 108
    World War II, 66, 98, 102 ff.
Waterways, 16
Weygand, General Max, 109
Wheat, 80
Wirtschaft und Statistik, 70
World War, First *and* Second. *See* Wars

Yugoslavia, 120

Zola, 63, 98